Citizens by Treaty:
Texts by Hispanic New Mexicans,
1846–1925

Citizens by Treaty

Texts by Hispanic New Mexicans, 1846–1925

EDITED AND TRANSLATED BY

A. Gabriel Meléndez

The Modern Language Association of America

New York   2025

© 2025 by The Modern Language Association of America
85 Broad Street, New York, New York 10004
www.mla.org

To order MLA publications, visit www.mla.org/books. For wholesale and
international orders, see www.mla.org/bookstore-orders. The EU-based
Responsible Person for MLA products is the Mare Nostrum Group, which
can be reached at gpsr@mare-nostrum.co.uk or the Mare Nostrum Group BV,
Mauritskade 21D, 1091 GC Amsterdam, Netherlands. For a copy of the MLA's
risk assessment document, write to scholcomm@mla.org.

The MLA office is located on the island known as Mannahatta (Manhattan) in
Lenapehoking, the homeland of the Lenape people. The MLA pays respect to the
original stewards of this land and to the diverse and vibrant Native communities
that continue to thrive in New York City.

Cover illustration: *Gentle Healing*, by Janie Perry Gonzales, Albuquerque,
New Mexico.

"To the Homeland" was originally published in *The Writings of Eusebio Chacón*,
edited and translated by A. Gabriel Meléndez and Francisco Lomelí (University
of New Mexico Press, 2012). "Ode to the Heroes" and "To Miss Adelina Otero-
Warren" were originally published in *El feliz ingenio neomexicano: Felipe M. Chacón
and* Poesía y prosa, edited and translated by Anna M. Nogar and A. Gabriel
Meléndez (University of New Mexico Press, 2021). These texts are reproduced
here courtesy of the University of New Mexico Press.

Texts and Translations 46
ISSN 1079-2538

Library of Congress Cataloging-in-Publication Data

Names: Meléndez, A. Gabriel (Anthony Gabriel), editor, translator.
Title: Citizens by treaty : texts by Hispanic New Mexicans, 1846-1925 / edited and
    translated by A. Gabriel Meléndez.
Other titles: Ciudadanos por tratado. English
Description: New York : The Modern Language Association of America, 2025.
Series: Texts and translations, 1079-2538 ; 46 | Includes bibliographical references.
Identifiers: LCCN 2024053303 (print) | LCCN 2024053304 (ebook) |
    ISBN 9781603296946 (paperback) | ISBN 9781603296953 (EPUB)
Subjects: LCSH: Mexicans—Southwest, New—History—Sources. | Mexican
    Americans—Southwest, New—History—Sources. | Southwest, New—
    History—Sources. | Southwest, New—Social life and customs—Sources. |
    Spanish language—Southwest, New—History—Sources.
Classification: LCC F790.M5 C5813 2025 (print) | LCC F790.M5 (ebook) |
    DDC 979/.02—dc23/eng20250207
LC record available at https://lccn.loc.gov/2024053303
LC ebook record available at https://lccn.loc.gov/2024053304

Contents

VII. The Piece of Earth We Love

VIII. On the Graves of Our Ancestors

Introduction

The day after Brigadier General Stephen Watts Kearny, at the head of the Army of the West, took New Mexico and other territories in what is today the US Southwest by military annexation, the interim Mexican governor of New Mexico, Juan Bautista Vigil y Alarid, impelled by duty, addressed a crowd of conquered New Mexicans that had assembled at the plaza of Santa Fe to hear his remarks. Vigil y Alarid delivered a strained, carefully worded proclamation of allegiance to the general and to his soldiers and the nation that had sent them west.

Vigil y Alarid's speech, delivered at the very moment of Kearny's arrival in 1846, is a remarkable statement that is at once measured and full of resonant irony. The speech would prove to be prophetic, a harbinger for those assembled, and with implications that would cascade down to future generations.

Kearny also made strategic use of the two proclamations he issued to the residents of New Mexico, the first at Las Vegas, New Mexico, on 15 August 1846, and the second, once his troops had entered Santa Fe four days later, on 19 August. In Las Vegas, Kearny was still not certain of what kind of military battle the Nuevomexicanos, the Mexican residents of New Mexico, might or could wage against his troops in the days to follow. Directing his announcement to the *alcalde*, or mayor, he immediately moved to deter any resistance from the Mexicans, saying:

> Mr. Alcalde, and people of New Mexico: I have come amongst you by the orders of my government, to take possession of your country, and extend over it the laws of the United States. We consider it, and have done so for some time, a part of the territory of the United States. We come amongst you as friends—not as enemies; as protectors—not as conquerors. We come among you for your benefit—not for your injury. Henceforth I absolve you from all allegiance to the Mexican government, and from all obedience to General Armijo. He is no longer your governor. . . . I am your governor.   (qtd. in Weber 161)

At Las Vegas he in no uncertain terms spoke to those who would raise up arms against him: "he who promises to be quiet, and is found in arms against me, I will hang!" (qtd. in Weber 161–62). After entering Santa Fe, the New Mexican capital, Kearny repeated portions of his Las Vegas speech and went on to name Vigil y Alarid as the interim authority to oversee domestic matters in New Mexico.[1]

Faced with inevitable change, Vigil y Alarid stood resolute, even as the authority of Mexico vanished before his eyes. On the one hand, he voiced appeasement and, on the other, he encouraged resoluteness, a dual move that blurred the lines between the old political reality and an emerging new political reality. His words, carefully parsed, addressed each segment of the assembled crowd. Turning to his neighbors, the residents of Santa Fe, he calmly advised, "A nosotros no nos toca decidir los límites de las naciones. Los gabinetes de Washington y México arreglarán sus diferencias" ("It is not for us to determine the boundaries of nations. The governments of Mexico and Washington will arrange these differences"). Standing before Kearny, he stated the obvious truth of the day without the least hint of sarcasm, "Nadie en este mundo ha resistido con éxito el poder del más fuerte" ("No one in this world can successfully resist the power of him who is stronger"), and with self-assurance continued, "Usted no se extrañe que nosotros no hayamos manifestado alegría y entusiasmo al ver esta ciudad ocupada por sus fuerzas militares" ("Do not find it strange if there has been no manifestation of joy and enthusiasm in seeing this city occupied by your military forces"). Vigil y Alarid cautiously advised the Americans that they had an obligation to act civilly toward the conquered. He then altered the tenor of his speech as he tried to imagine what a future conjoined with Anglo-America might portend. His words were not clouded either by sycophancy or resentment, but rather, they denoted a clear-eyed recognition that inevitable consequences would follow that day. Again, speaking directly to each of his fellow Nuevomexicanos, he urged them to view things with confidence and determination so that they might remain fiercely attached to their homeland and to their way of life, even at a moment when an unknowable future awaited them. The turn was as sharp as it was clear: "Para nosotros ha muerto el poder de la república mexicana. Ella, seáse cuál fueran sus circumstancias era nuestra madre" ("The power of the Mexican republic is now dead to us. No matter what Mexico's condition may have been, she was our mother").

Vigil y Alarid was one of a small but significant number of Nuevomexicanos who in the parlance of the time would have been deemed *letrados*, persons of letters who had some amount of formal education. Prior to the departure of Manuel Armijo, the last Mexican governor of New Mexico, Vigil y Alarid had served as the secretary to the governor for the provincial department. At the time of his birth, New Mexico was still a part of New Spain, the colonial viceroyalty encompassing what is to today Central America, Mexico, and as far north as Colorado. His career as a bureaucrat spanned the entirety of the twenty-five years that New Mexico was part of the republic of Mexico. In this capacity, he would have continually been tasked with writing reports, keeping records, and issuing correspondence for the provincial authorities in Santa Fe. Many of his *vecinos*, or neighbors, in provincial New Mexico would not have possessed his same skills in the art of writing and would not have been considered people of letters. That being said, many of those neighbors would have been practiced in the verbal arts and would have engaged in public displays of oratory, declamations of verse, funerary oration, ritual ceremonies, and storytelling intended to educate assembled listeners. They were equally people of the word and stood by what they declared in public and in private. In contrast to his *vecinos*, Vigil y Alarid was expected to be dexterous in the oral and manuscript culture of his day and time. (Scholars of New Mexico history have discussed Vigil y Alarid's public address [Padilla; Sisneros].) Following the US military annexation of the Southwest, the lettered and unlettered, the tutored and the autodidacts, compelled themselves to press forward and express their views by whatever expressive means remained open to them. This collection, *Ciudadanos por tratado* (*Citizens by Treaty*), reflects the legacy of both groups in the verbal arts.

Citizens by Treaty is a collection of texts that gives voice to a segment of the US citizenry whose cultural and literary legacy has gone largely unrecognized. This anthology compiles works of different genres produced by US citizens of Mexican descent whose immediate and distant ancestors resided in New Mexico, Arizona, California, Texas, and Colorado prior to the incorporation of these regions into the United States. Though scattered across a geographically immense region, the writers shared a common language and culture that had developed and adapted itself to the region over three centuries. Following the Mexican-American War, Mexicans became citizens of the United States by virtue of the Treaty of Guadalupe Hidalgo, an international accord signed and ratified in 1848 by the United States and the republic of Mexico. In the long struggle toward the full inclusion of ethnic minorities in the body politic of the United States, Mexican Americans stand out as the only group of considerable size in US history to have had their rights as citizens inscribed in legal terms and guaranteed by international treaty. Rosina Lozano notes that citizenship for Mexican Americans preceded that of African Americans by two decades. Formerly enslaved individuals became citizens as a consequence of the ratification of the Fourteenth Amendment to the US Constitution. Lozano further concludes, "Treaty citizens were the first geographically dispersed, politically significant and racially ambiguous group to gain U.S. citizenship" (6).

In referencing this population, I invoke the descriptor "treaty citizens," as employed by Lozano in her masterful book *An American Language: The History of Spanish in the United States*. This term, woven into the title of this anthology, is meant to underscore the inevitable consternation felt by this population in its attempt to negotiate a new national affiliation. Citizenship and belonging forged by the stipulations of an international treaty in turn produced a modality of thought that underpins the style and substance of the writings that form this collection, most of which speak to the destabilizing predicament of loyalty versus allegiance amid cultural, political, social, economic, religious, and linguistic disruption.

The term "treaty citizens" provides an important legal-political descriptor that I find helpful in understanding the significance of the texts in this collection. This said, it is critically important to recognize that a variety of ethnic labels have been used historically to describe the Hispanic population of the United States, beginning with the umbrella terms *Hispanic, Latino,* and *Latina.* There is no simple way to deal with the complexity of nomenclature when considering this group.

The Nature of the Works

Over years and across decades, treaty citizens, both men and women, gave expression to their experiences by inscribing their thoughts, passions, and aspirations and sharing them in oral performance and in written texts. They transmitted their lived experiences and exchanged the fruits of their imagination across various genres using the venues at their disposal. They continued to make use of the manuscript culture and to perform the vibrant and expressive oral tradition they had inherited from colonial New Spain and Mexico. When no other means were available, they placed their folk dramas, prayers, popular verses (*versos de arte menor*), and loftier verses (*versos de arte mayor*) in ledger books, where their compositions took the form of diaries, personal breviaries, and point-counterpoint dialogues, known as *coloquios.* In time they would come to employ the discipline and the habits of mind of scribes who were bold enough to commit their thoughts to print. With the advent of typographic presses and after managing to establish weekly newspapers in several towns across the region, treaty citizens were determined to share the full panoply of their literary and cultural concerns with a growing group of newspaper readers. As printing and publishing became more available, literary works of all kinds began to populate Spanish-language newspapers, which regularly featured editorial essays, short novels in serial form, historical tracts, biographies, poetry, political satire, opinion columns, and contestations of various sorts that gave voice to racial, linguistic, religious, and civil rights grievances. The importance of the Spanish-language press, as I have described elsewhere, was decisive:

> The multiple functions of the Mexicano newspaper presses resulted in the publication of "culture bearing" documentation wherein are found cultural projections of every kind in prose, poetry, and the editorial essay. Newspapers became the principal means for Nuevomexicanos to tap the wellspring of their Indo-Hispano literary and expressive sensibility and share it publicly via the printed word. (Meléndez 7)

The writings in this collection appeared at a time marked by the confluence of tradition and change, at a time when treaty citizens began to collectively contemplate what would become of their lands and possessions; what rights they would have under the new government; what would become of their language, their livelihoods, their religion, and their history; what future they would bequeath to their offspring; and whether they would continue to have a place in the public sphere and in the civic and cultural life of their homeland. The most active decades of the Spanish-language press coincide with a series of historical moments that dramatically affected treaty citizens: Treaty citizens would live through sixty-two years of territorial rule. They would experience the arrival of the railroad, the telegraph, film, and radio. They would fight in the American Civil War, the Spanish-American War, and World War I. And they would see Arizona and New Mexico gain statehood in 1912.

The Significance of the Works

The literary works of treaty citizens cannot be labeled as immigrant literature produced by individuals who had one foot in a home country and another in the United States. The chief concerns of treaty citizens revolved around what the future held for them in the land of their birth—that is, in their ancestral homeland. Not having the option to return to a sending country like Mexico or another Latin America nation, these writers oscillate between reproducing and reinjecting vitality into cultural expressions inherited from established oral narrative and manuscript traditions and addressing the effects of loss and uprootedness stemming from the condition of being relegated to second-class citizenship. These writings are powerful for the tenacity they exhibit and for the sense of belonging they claim. Many express the quality of *querencia*,[2] an abiding attachment to place, evoked as a means of counteracting the displacing effects of the US takeover of the West. Thus, these works are a sounding board for registering not only the grievances but also the hopes of a colonized minority in its own homeland.

The Works in Context

Since its founding in 1992, the project *Recovering the US Hispanic Literary Heritage*, based at the University of Houston, has been the focal point of a comprehensive scholarly endeavor whose mission has been to research, preserve, and disseminate the literary culture, broadly defined, of Latinos and Latinas in the United States from colonial times to 1960 (Kanellos et al. 4; Gutiérrez and Padilla 13). The project began with the recovery and inclusion of literary texts, mostly from Spanish sources, produced in areas of the United States that were at one time colonies of Spain or that later became part of the republic of Mexico and eventually became US territory at the end of the Mexican-American War. Setting 1960 as the end point of the project's work was not meant to exclude contemporary contributions spawned by the Chicano and Puerto Rican civil rights activism of the 1960s and 1970s; rather, it was a tacit acknowledgment that these movements were not in danger of being ignored by contemporary scholars. The project sought to dispel the notion that the Hispanic experience constituted a new phenomenon, one that had simply burst onto the scene out of nowhere. From the outset, the project took the view that unearthing the historical expressions of Latino and Latina culture was a necessary precursor to understanding the transnational outlook of these communities since earliest times. Writing in 2002, Nicolás Kanellos and his team of coeditors noted, "Hispanic peoples in the United States are the result of the United States expanding its borders, of concurring and incorporating and importing peoples from the Hispanic world, which has existed not only immediately outside but within the United States (29).

The work of building the archive of Latino and Latina textual production over time and over an immense geographic area, with the added goal of creating comprehensive databases, continues to be an enormous and ongoing undertaking. Twenty years into this work, *Recovering the US Hispanic Literary Heritage* realized an important goal with the publication of *Herencia: The Anthology of Hispanic Literature of the United States*, edited by Kanellos and colleagues. The sheer volume of texts (colonial times to the present) to be included in *Herencia* required a careful partitioning of the larger whole. The collection came to encompass three sections ("Native Literature," "Literature of Immigration," and "Literature of Exile") in order to accommodate the scope and chronology of this legacy. The sections on immigration and exile include works representative of the Puerto Rican and Cuban experience conditioned by periods of immigration or political upheaval, while the section on native literature acknowledges literary traditions that took root in regions that were originally part of Spain and Mexico. It is this section that concerns me here. First, the use of *native* to describe this corpus needs some further explanation, considering that the term has become synonymous with indigeneity. Above all, for Kanellos and his coeditors, the term denotes rootedness: "Hispanic native literature developed an ethnic minority literature first among Hispanics already residing in the Southwest when the United States appropriated it from Mexico" (5). In many ways the term denotes the tenacity of expressive culture (in Spanish), rooted in specific places and developing under particular circumstances.

After 1848, several distinct populations continued to reside in areas that became US possessions. They included not only members of Native American tribes but also mestizos who claimed regional affinities as Tejanos (Mexican residents of Texas), Californios (Mexican residents of California), Tucsonenses (Mexican residents of southern Arizona), and Nuevomexicanos (Mexican residents of New Mexico). Hispanics in New Mexico, Texas, Arizona, and California attempted to keep their culture intact and to respond to their predicament as conquered citizens. The Spanish-language newspapers they founded produced a sizable textual presence in the former Mexican areas of the Southwest.

Works by descendants of the settlers of Mexican California include the writings of Mariano Guadalupe Vallejo and the first English-language novels, *Who Would Have Thought It* and *The Squatter and the Don*, written by María Amparo Ruíz de Burton. The first memoir in English, by the Tejano

Juan Nepomuceno Seguín, provides an eyewitness account of events leading up to the Battle of the Alamo in Texas.

The texts gathered in *Citizens by Treaty* fall under the designation of "native literature," as employed in the *Herencia* anthology. For a variety of reasons, Nuevomexicanos managed to retain their cultural identity and to express themselves in ways that contrast to some degree with the literary legacy of other treaty citizens. This is largely due to the early and sustained presence of the Nuevomexicanos in a region they considered their homeland, a feature that set the course for a distinct version of events in the Southwest, as Kanellos and his coeditors note:

> Only in New Mexico did Hispanics maintain a demographic superiority in the late nineteenth and twentieth centuries—New Mexico was the territory that first developed a widespread independent native Hispanic press and sustained it well into the twentieth century. Not only did more Hispanics than Anglos live there, they resided in a more compact area and with comparatively less competition and violence from Anglo newcomers. The Nuevomexicanos were able to hold on to more lands, property and institutions than did the Hispanics of California or Texas. Control of their own newspapers and publications became essential in the eyes of Hispanic intellectuals and community leaders in the development of Nuevomexicano identity and self-determination in the face of adjusting to a new culture foisted upon them during the territorial period. (8)

The self-determination of the Nuevomexicanos and their participation in politics, education, and social life also made it possible for the group to continue to maintain its religious observances and cultural practices with relatively little change over time. In drawing on this specific legacy, *Citizens by Treaty* seeks to illustrate the tenacity of Hispanic expressive culture in New Mexico, the area where it operated most continuously and where it has left an indelible mark.

Owing to the early founding of Spanish-Mexican settlements in the West—Santa Fe (1608), San Antonio (1718), Tucson (1775), Los Angeles (1781)—that proceeded from several centuries of Spanish rule, treaty citizens, while racially heterogeneous, saw themselves as inheritors of both Iberian and New World cultures, and, thus, they thought, wrote, and expressed themselves in the Spanish language. As inheritors of books and learning that passed from one generation to the next through written and oral traditions, the writings they produced after 1846 derive from older traditions and modes of expression.

Among the territories acquired by the United States after the Mexican-American War, New Mexico stands apart from other regions for a number of historical and sociological reasons. For one, it is the region that produced the most pronounced tradition of writing from treaty citizens, in part because New Mexico had the largest concentration of former Mexican citizens, and because they continued to exert influence in their ancestral homeland. In the years immediately following the acquisition of New Mexico by the United States, Nuevomexicanos made up some eighty-five percent of the citizenry of the territory. After 1848 New Mexico received far fewer English-speaking immigrants from other parts of the United States than did California or Texas, and it was the only place where Hispanics maintained numerical superiority throughout a half century of territorial rule. It was also a region where established patterns in daily customs, religious practices, community observances, foodways, and folk celebrations continued to be practiced without being altered by outside influences. Equally remarkable, as Lozano suggests,

> [t]he territory of New Mexico is the sole example of a Spanish-dominated political and legislative system in the continental United States. Monolingual Spanish-speaking citizens became accustomed to being addressed in their mother tongue in speeches, newspapers, and campaign appeals. In return for their participation in elections and party loyalty, Nuevomexicanos secured local patronage positions and favors for their small villages and towns, where most of their true allegiances lay. (100)

Through the Spanish-language press and through participation in electoral politics, Nuevomexicanos managed to keep a presence in the public square, and their writings stand as an early case of cultural pluralism and a rare model for ethnic and social integration in the United States.

Style and Aesthetics

The salient characteristic of writings by treaty citizens is the strident urgency with which they are produced. In speech acts both oral and written, equal measures of consternation, denunciation, resistance, and affirmation are voiced. Urgency not only fuels social and political denunciation and declamation but also steadies these writings as an undertone, especially when quiet elegance is called for in rendering affirmations on history, family, religion, work, personal responsibility, and similar topics. Likewise, declamation and reclamation in the face of uncertainty to one degree or another shapes these works of poetry, fiction, folk drama, historical chronicle, political satire, essay, epistle and ballads, biography, and memoir.

Compilation

Citizens by Treaty largely displays the literary expressions nested within the discursive culture fomented by Spanish-language newspaper publication in New Mexico across some six decades (1870–1930). It brings together materials that best illustrate the significance, modality, and aesthetic properties of the cultural program treaty citizens forged in defense of their history in the hope of building a more just and beneficial future for themselves and the nation that had enveloped them.

Over several decades I have identified and cataloged hundreds of representative texts, preparing some for publication and critically analyzing dozens more in scholarly writings. *Citizens by Treaty* conjoins materials I have previously taken to publication with a number of unpublished works. Together, these poems, *coloquios*, folk dramas, chronicles, political essays, epistles, and memoirs widen scholarly understanding of the literature and culture of treaty citizens. Each entry in the collection is introduced by a headnote. In some instances, one headnote introduces a cluster of texts that address the same theme.

The book includes entries by anonymous writers whose expressive thought is representative of the rich oral and ritual life that continues to be celebrated in villages and towns across the region. These expressions, penned by community members, take the form of popular verses; ballads, or *corridos*; tales, or *cuentos*; dramatic dialogues, or *trovas*; and folk dramas. These texts, which often began as oral performances, reveal the importance of an inherited tradition, one that newspaper editors referenced, reproduced, and valued in defense of a way of life that was under threat of erasure and excision and as a means for elaborating a native intellectual tradition.

The collection contains thirty-one entries divided into eight sections that illustrate several prevailing concerns expressed by treaty citizens across multiple decades. Sections are titled as follows: "México fue nuestra madre" ("Mexico Was Our Mother"), "Al improviso: Trovas, cantos, cuentos y bailes" ("Improvisation: Dialogues, Songs, Stories, and Dances"), "Nuevo México: Ni nuevo, ni México" ("New Mexico: Not New, Not Mexico"), "Ciudadanos sin reproche" ("Citizens beyond Reproach"), "Escuelas para las masas" ("Schools for the Masses"), "¿Qué idioma hablaremos?" ("What Language Will We Speak?"), "Terruño y querencia" ("The Piece of Earth We Love"), and "Sobre las tumbas de nuestros antepasados" ("On the Graves of Our Ancestors").

On the one hand, the label "treaty citizens" is helpful in denoting the demographic constituency whose works are found in this anthology. On the other hand, the term does not account for the diversity of ascriptive labels, self-ascribed or imposed, that over the course of decades have been employed to identify this population. Several ethnic labels appear and often are used interchangeably in the texts collected here. Consider, for example, that the Jesuit editors of *La Revista Católica* (*The Catholic Review*; entry 13) used "mexicano" ("Mexican"), "nuevomexicano" ("New Mexican"), and "neo-mexicano" ("neo-Mexican") in alternation when referring to the Spanish-speaking resident population of New Mexico. Other terms commonly used in these writings are "ciudadano nativo" ("native citizen"), "hispano" ("Hispanic"), and "hispanoamericano" ("Spanish American"). To the degree possible, I have elected to use *Nuevomexicano* as a default tag when referring to New Mexico's treaty citizens. For one thing, it is the most widely defused of the terms because it is the moniker of the longest-running Spanish-language newspaper in the region, Santa Fe's *El Nuevo Mexicano*, and also because of the way it bonds the associative identity of a land-based people to the very geography they inhabit, a matter of paramount importance to this population.

The decision to open this collection with Vigil y Alarid's pronouncement of 1846 was a straightforward one. Determining when to close the anthology was somewhat more problematic because it is not entirely clear when, or even if, the Nuevomexicanos were ever fully removed from public, civic, and cultural life in New Mexico. Paul Horgan's observations about Santa Fe in the 1920s provide insight into the crosscurrents of social life in the New Mexican capital in the years after New Mexico gained statehood. Before 1920, Horgan writes, Santa Fe was still a small town, and "its character was largely Mexican" (310). Its "living energies," he notes, came largely from its Hispanic residents, who contributed to the town's business life, politics, and municipal and state government work. Those energies were most palpable at regular sessions of the state legislature, when "[f]rom all corners of the immense state came cattlemen and sheep ranchers, businessmen and lawyers, as elected representatives of the people of New Mexico. Here was always a chance for a particularly developed Latin talent to express itself" (324). By 1930 regular sessions of the legislature had dispensed with bilingual (i.e., English-and-Spanish) proceedings and with spoken interpretation, a positive development in Horgan's estimation. While Horgan considers the former language requirement to have been an obstacle to the efficient transaction of business (324), surely the Hispanic citizenry of the state did not view the removal of Spanish from this most prized public institution with the same enthusiasm. Treaty citizens continued to speak their native language and display their expressive culture in plazas, streets, restaurants, hotels, and churches; on public school playgrounds; at voting precincts; and at civic gatherings.

While the entries in *Citizens by Treaty* are arranged thematically, I would point readers to the terminus that an anonymous poem dedicated to the city of Santa Fe (entry 27) and an essay by a Santa Fe resident, Luz Elena Ortiz (entry 28), provide this collection. These texts appear at a time when several key issues were still in play in New Mexico and when Camilo Padilla's *Revista Ilustrada (Illustrated Review)* continued to give voice to the literary and artistic works of treaty citizens. Both pieces attest to the determination of treaty citizens to fully exercise their right to civic participation and express their profound attachment to New Mexico as a homeland. While such writings continued to be produced and circulated in Spanish, it is also true that the culture that produced them would come to experience greater political, economic, and social distress in the 1930s and beyond. In time, the forces of change and imposition would dislodge Nuevomexicanos from the center of life in the state and remainder them to the sidelines of public life in the region.

Notes

1. While no published version of Kearny's Santa Fe proclamation is available, in describing the Las Vegas speech, the historian David J. Weber notes, "Kearny's proclamation at Las Vegas made strong assurances—even to the point of guaranteeing United States protection against Indians. Kearny was to make similar assurances in the plaza at Santa Fe on August 19 and 22" (161).

2. This sense of rootedness and identification with place survives in the barrios in villages and in the conversations and reflections of present-day Nuevomexicanos, as evidenced by the publication of the anthology *Querencia: Reflections on the New Mexico Homeland* in 2020 (Fonseca-Chávez et al.).

Works Cited

Fonseca-Chávez, Vanessa, et al., editors. *Querencia: Reflections on the New Mexico Homeland.* U of New Mexico P, 2020.

Gutiérrez, Ramón, and Genaro Padilla, editors. *Recovering the US Hispanic Literary Heritage.* Arte Público Press, 1993.

Horgan, Paul. *The Centuries of Santa Fe.* U of New Mexico P, 1984.

Kanellos, Nicolás, et al., editors. *Herencia: The Anthology of Hispanic Literature of the United States.* Oxford UP, 2002.

Lozano, Rosina. *An American Language: The History of Spanish in the United States.* U of California P, 2018.

Meléndez, A. Gabriel. *So All Is Not Lost: The Poetics of Print in Nuevomexicano Communities, 1834–1958.* U of New Mexico P, 1997.

Padilla, Genaro. *My History, Not Yours: The Formation of Mexican American Autobiography.* U of Wisconsin P, 2002.

Sisneros, Samuel E. "'She Was Our Mother': New Mexico's Change of National Sovereignty and Juan Bautista Vigil y Alarid, the Last Mexican Governor of New Mexico." *All Trails Lead to Santa Fe: An Anthology Commemorating the Four-Hundredth Anniversary of the Founding of Santa Fe in 1619,* Sunstone Press, 2010, pp. 279–97.

Weber, David J., editor. *Foreigners in Their Native Land: Historical Roots of Mexican Americans.* U of New Mexico P, 1973.

Note on the Translation

In translating these materials, I have taken great care in ensuring that their meaning reflects that of the original Spanish. Since the Spanish of New Mexico exhibits certain characteristics that distinguish it from other dialects spoken in Mexico and Spain, I have been mindful of this as well. The chief distinctions derive from the retention of archaic vocabulary that no longer has currency in standard Spanish, such as the use of *estafeta* for *oficina de correos* ("post office"), *alverjón* for *guisantes* ("peas"), and *anteojos de larga vista* for *binoculares* ("binoculars"). Similarly, some phonological mannerisms are holdovers from the Spanish introduced in the region in the sixteenth and seventeenth centuries. For example, the aspiration of *f*, *s*, and *h* renders *jui* for *fui* ("I went"), *jervir* for *hervir* ("to boil"), and so on. Certain verb forms differ from those employed in standard Spanish. For example, the verb endings in the second-person plural *hablaste* ("you spoke") and *fuiste* ("you went") are rendered as *hablates* and *fuites*. Likewise, with verbs such as *ver* ("to see") and *traer* ("to bring"), variations appear in certain conjugations: for example, *vide* ("I saw") for *vi*, *truje* ("I brought") for *traje*, and *trujimos* ("we brought") for *trajimos*. Over time a number of words borrowed from English, or anglicisms (see entries 24–26), would add a distinct feature to Spanish as spoken across the Southwest.

When needed, clarifications are provided in brackets or endnotes. At every turn I have worked to make clear to English readers the extent to which the Spanish originals conform to the poetic and stylistic registers of the time in which they were produced. In rendering the English translations, I have relied on my skills as a bilingual writer, employing much of what I learned when writing The Book of Archives *and Other Stories from the Mora Valley, New Mexico* (2017), where my work as a translator retains the rigor of archival research and the creative spirit of imaginative writing.

Citizens by Treaty

I. Mexico Was Our Mother

1. "General, Sir," Juan Bautista Vigil y Alarid

19 August 1846, Santa Fe, New Mexico

Given within days of the entrance of US troops into New Mexico at the start of the Mexican-American War, "Señor General" ("General, Sir") is the speech delivered by the interim governor of New Mexico, Juan Bautista Vigil y Alarid, to Brigadier General Stephen Watts Kearny and the assembled residents of Santa Fe in August 1846. The speech was delivered in response to the proclamation issued by General Kearny on the plaza in Santa Fe, New Mexico. Kearny's proclamations called on the residents of New Mexico to declare allegiance to the United States. Vigil y Alarid's carefully constructed reply would prove to be declarative, symbolic, and prophetic, with far-reaching implications for what was to become the permanent disposition of all future relationships between the former citizens of the Mexican republic and their new American occupiers. Facing inevitable change, Vigil y Alarid confronts the moment and strikes a balance between appeasement and resistance. The conditions of the US takeover of the Southwest would persist in time and affect the descendants of the people Vigil y Alarid addressed in Santa Fe in August 1846. The original text survives as a facsimile of the document penned and signed by Vigil y Alarid and later incorporated into Ralph Emerson Twitchell's classic work, *The History of the Military Occupation of the Territory of New Mexico from 1846 to 1851 by the Government of the United*

States.[1] For more on Vigil y Alarid's public and personal affairs, see Sisneros 281–83; Padilla 43–51.

Works Cited

Padilla, Genaro. *My History, Not Yours: The Formation of Mexican American Autobiography.* U of Wisconsin P, 2002.

Sisneros, Samuel E. "'She Was Our Mother': New Mexico's Change of National Sovereignty and Juan Bautista Vigil y Alarid, the Last Mexican Governor of New Mexico." *All Trails Lead to Santa Fe: An Anthology Commemorating the Four-Hundredth Anniversary of the Founding of Santa Fe in 1619,* Sunstone Press, 2010, pp. 279–97.

Twitchell, Ralph Emerson. *The History of the Military Occupation of the Territory of New Mexico from 1846 to 1851 by the Government of the United States.* Smith-Brooks, 1909.

General, Sir

General: The address which you have just delivered, in which you announce that you have taken possession of this great country in the name of the United States of America, gives us some idea of the great future that awaits us. It is not for us to determine the boundaries of nations. The governments of Mexico and Washington will arrange these differences. It is for us to obey and respect the established authorities, no matter what our opinions as private citizens may be. The inhabitants of this department humbly and honorably present their loyalty and allegiance to the government of North America. No one in this world can successfully resist the power of him who is stronger. Do not find it strange if there has been no manifestation of joy and enthusiasm in seeing this city occupied by your military forces. The power of the Mexican republic is now dead to us. No matter what Mexico's condition may have been, she was our mother. What child will not shed abundant tears at the tomb of his parents? Although I might indicate some of the causes of her misfortunes, domestic troubles should not be made public. It is sufficient to say that civil war is the cursed source of the deadly poison which has spread over one of the grandest and greatest countries ever created. Today we belong to a great and powerful nation. Its flag, with its stars and stripes, swathes the horizon of New Mexico, and its brilliant light shines on this land, and falls on tender seeds, now planted in fertile ground which, if well cultivated, shall propagate. We are cognizant of your kindness, of your courtesy and that of your accompanying officers, and of the strict discipline of your troops;[2] we know that we belong to the republic that owes its origin to the immortal Washington, whom all civilized nations admire and respect. How different would be our situation had we been invaded by European nations! We are aware of the unfortunate condition of the Poles.[3] In the name, then, of this entire department, I swear obedience to the northern republic and tender my respect to its laws and authority.

2. "To the Homeland," Eusebio Chacón

El Boletín Popular, vol. 12, no. 52, 7 October 1897,
Santa Fe, New Mexico

In "A la patria" ("To the Homeland"), Eusebio Chacón
(1870–1948) employs more formal metric forms associated
with *versos de arte mayor*, Spanish poetry thought to con-
stitute high art. Chacón distills his ode to Mexico in the
form of an *octava real*, a poetic form consisting of eight-line
stanzas and eleven-syllable verses unified by a tight conso-
nantal rhyme scheme. The poem reflects several stylistic
conventions drawn from Latin American modernist and
neoromantic aesthetics, then in vogue. The poet aims to
evoke lexical complexity, eschewing everyday speech in
favor of lyrical and sensorial language. Likewise, his im-
ages often rest on classical Greek and Roman tropes, even
as he attempts to elevate Mesoamerican origins and sym-
bolism. From this emerges an expressive tension that is not
fully resolved, as can be seen, for example, in stanza 11, in
verses that juxtapose Ceres, the Roman goddess of agricul-
ture, and the native Mexican staple agave.

The poem reflects Chacón's understanding of the his-
torical rupture produced by the American takeover of
New Mexico. The break, in essence, split Mexico in two,
with Chacón's place of birth becoming part of the United
States. Chacón's poetic allusions, drawn from history, in-
tersect with the social circumstances the poet faces in his
own time and allow for a lyrical retracing of the deep psy-
chological scars that had begun to disfigure Nuevomexi-
canos' sense of a cultural self. Published some fifty years
after New Mexico had ceased to be a part of the Mexican
republic, the poem is a surprising reflection on the deep
ties between Mexico and her former territories, made pre-
sent as Chacón inserts his awareness of his family's partici-
pation in events in Mexican history. Equally remarkable
is the introspection found in the poem because it plumbs

the ramifications felt even into Chacón's generation of
the historical break occasioned by the Mexican-American
War and the continuing dispossession it occasioned for the
Nuevomexicanos. For Chacón and members of his genera-
tion, questions of dispossession continued to play out in
the daily relations between Nuevomexicanos and newly
arriving Anglo-Americans in the reconfigured lands of the
Southwest.

For more on Chacón as a central figure in the literary
arts movement that emerged from the vibrant Spanish-
language press of the 1890s and as a leading exponent of a
literary movement he came to term "una literatura nacio-
nal" ("a national literature"), see Meléndez 133–37, 144–54;
Meléndez and Lomelí 1–24. For more on Chacón and Nue-
vomexicano identity, see Nieto-Phillips 14–17.

Works Cited

Meléndez, A. Gabriel. *So All Is Not Lost: The Poetics of Print in
    Nuevomexicano Communities, 1834–1958*. U of New Mexico P,
    1997.

Meléndez, A. Gabriel, and Francisco Lomelí, editors and
    translators. *The Writings of Eusebio Chacón*. U of New Mexico
    P, 2012.

Nieto-Phillips, John. *The Language of Blood: The Making of
    Spanish American Identity in the Southwest*. U of New Mexico P,
    2004.

To the Homeland

Upright land of giant nopal,[4]

Where Cortez's genius opened its wings,

Regal home of La Malinche,[5]

Land of beautiful flowers and wonders,

You stand by the roaring sea

As it bathes your virgin feet and you

Bestow in return a green seaside and scented winds
Oh, fill my thoughts with love of country.

I was not born in the nest made
by the valiant eagles that formed you,
And while my fathers fought for your honor
And died in glorious battle for you,
I was born under those who humbled you,
Those who placed a boot on your neck,
I was born under those that took from you,
Unblemished Mexico, the land that I love.

Still, I press forward in my exile,
Unsure of the path to come,
If you cry out, I too cry out, dear friend
If you laugh, I shall meet you with my joy;
In the victory march, I stand with you.
My banners waving in the wind
But, should your face be shrouded with pain
Your sorrow will envelop my being.

Today, your forehead crowned
by the olive branches from the victory at Puebla,[6]
My faith for your future is revived,
For you have mastered a fateful course,
You, born from peaceful rebellion,
And in time you have grown strong,

Sword in hand, you claim your destiny,
And the peace that lies ahead is full of promise.

The regal flowers in your gardens
Turn the autumn sun into fragrant, golden
Blossoms that sway in the zephyrs
While under some old tree a mighty sword swings,
Suddenly filled with these gifts
your steep foothills, now dark and dry, will
Turn to gold, bright like a gentle smile,
That emerges deep from your bosom.

The tyrants eyed your grandeur, saw your
Beauty from far across the seas
And they launched their unholy ships,
And seized you with bloody hands,
Offering liberty as a torch
Even as they reign supreme in crime,
And from your maternal arms they tore
Away the laws your founders made.

Frightened, your many eagles
Beat their wings and took flight
Scouring the desolate sandbanks for
Peace, comfort, and asylum.
They perch silently before your misfortune
And seeing you as a slave in your own land

They bend down their once proud beaks
Muffled is the song of your past glories.

Night found you seated,
At a lonely and beautiful breaker
Pondering the foam of rushing waves,
Seeking in reflected droplets of ocean water,
the portrait of a yellow moon,
Or perhaps, in the fugitive flash of the starlight
Cast to earth from the star of hope, like the promise
Of mercy that reaches the deepest source of pain.

Suddenly your warrior offspring,
Those noble armies set for battle
Stand before the battlefield fires,
Before all hope evaporates,
Rush to your aid in massive waves,
Fierce and menacing they encircle the enemy
And they raise up your shield, and cry:
"Take up the cause, for the country calls!"

"Take up the cause," sons of Mars,[7]
The second of April is a glorious day,
Let loose the bombs on the imperial caste;
Make the cannons roar and cast off the useless sloth,
Rail against the acts that seduced, the mercenary,
    Miramar[8]

That claimed another victim,
Where in Carlota's[9] sumptuous palace,
A woman laments her misfortune.

You had barely known the open sea
Where the squadron's colors so proudly
Broke upon the empty beaches,
While destiny rushed against you
You traded the sword for the sickle
And Ceres[10] gave, as at the dawn of time,
Brings forth cotton and sheaves of wheat
And the treasure of your agave[11] plant.

Oh, my homeland, why have I never known
What it is like to live on your precious soil?
My fate has been to live without your healing waters,
Never able to take a breath of your air.
What would it be like to inhale your life-giving
Winds? To avidly drink until full of
Your sweet waters?
Why? Please tell me?

What crime have I committed against you?
Must my lute always remain silent? Masking its
    harmonies,
And never shall the gentle north winds carry,
The melancholy echo of my song for you?

The wreath is broken, I shall bid adieu in tears
I go forth with such immense nostalgia,
A budding sorrow that grows in my spirit
And deferring my hopes and dreams.

II. Improvisation: Dialogues, Songs, Stories, and Dances

3. "Improvised Dialogues," from the oral tradition, Francisco Sena, Los Torres, New Mexico, 24 June 1975

Las Vegas Carnegie Public Library, Carnegie
Bicentennial Oral History Collection, Interview #22

These dramatic dialogues come from an oral interview given by Francisco Sena on 24 June 1975.[12] Sena informs the interviewer that he is eighty-eight years old and was born in the village of Los Torres, New Mexico, on 2 April 1887. The interview rescues knowledge of verbal performances that he witnessed as a child. Sena's recitations attest to the survival of oral performance narratives originating in New Mexico's colonial period and show how they were maintained with a high degree of integrity into the middle of the twentieth century, surviving long enough to be recorded as part of a Carnegie Library initiative marking the Bicentennial of the United States in 1976. Sena's dialogues are patterned after the *trovas* (verbal jousts in song) and *coloquios* (dialogues) of such legendary bards as El Viejo Vilmas (Old Man Vilmas), El Negro Poeta (the Black Poet), Gracia, Chicoria, and others of equal fame. The tradition of verse improvisations was meant to showcase a participant's command of oratory through displays of theological, moral, and philosophical knowledge designed to entertain and catechize assembled listeners. Across generations the most beloved verbal jousts were passed down and honored through recitation and reperformance.

In 1914, Aurelio M. Espinosa,[13] the preeminent philologist and scholar of Nuevomexicano folklore at the time, published four *trovas* "taken down from oral dictation" (105). Espinosa collected the compositions of Spanish-speaking residents of southern Colorado and northern New Mexico and transcribed them by hand prior to the widespread availability of recording technology. Three versions correspond to the cycle of verbal duels between Old Man Vilmas and the Black Poet; the fourth is an example of Vilmas facing off with Gracia. Although Espinosa estimated that the versions were not complete, he was impressed that his informants, relying on memory alone, had managed to provide versions containing thirty or more stanzas. Espinosa proffered that the *trova* had been an extremely popular form of popular entertainment, writing, "[T]here are very few New Mexicans over fifty years of age who cannot recite from memory one or more strophes of the compositions" (105). Espinosa also attempted to cull together what could be surmised about the historicity of the legendary bards Old Man Vilmas, the Black Poet, and Gracia.

Likely hampered by memory and the further erosion of the *trova* tradition, Sena's 1975 versions have fewer stanzas than those Espinosa documented, and the versification of his *trovas* is not entirely uniform, occasioning variability in the recitation of both verses and stanzas.

Trovadores ("troubadours") employed the *décima*, the most adaptable verse form in the *arte menor*, or vernacular register of verse making. *Décimas* consisted of ten-line strophes marked out in eight-syllable verses with a consonantal rhyming scheme. The *décima* was prized for the great dexterity it demanded of practitioners. How well the *décima* was executed distinguished a mature bard from an apprentice. The verbal jousts were often triggered by an initial *reto*, or challenge that sets in motion the point-counterpoint exchange of the ensuing declamations. Many times, the challenge was issued by one bard voicing a *planta*, or *verso de pie forzado* ("the required verse"), which required the challenger to create new verses to follow the *planta* while maintaining the flourish required by the established rhyme scheme. Beyond the recitation of these dialogues, Sena also recites the freestanding piece "La décima de los reyes" ("The Décima of the Kings"). The poem is filled with allusions drawn from myths of antiquity and, as such, presents a marvelous example of the most unexpected themes coming into the repertoire of verse makers in the remote villages of New Mexico. Remarkable, too, is how Sena was able to recall something of the structure and poetics of these compositions, thus providing insight on how the art of the *trova* was transmitted to him as a young man. For more information on Espinosa, see Nieto-Phillips 178–79, 183–87.

Works Cited

Espinosa, Aurelio M. "New Mexico Spanish Folklore." *The Journal of American Folklore*, vol. 27, no. 104, Apr.-June 1914, pp. 105–47.

Nieto-Phillips, John. *The Language of Blood: The Making of Spanish American Identity in the Southwest*. U of New Mexico P, 2004.

Improvised Dialogues

Well, from what I have been able to learn, these were two bards that met in Mexico: Old Man Vilmas and the Black Poet.[14] *When they met, one began:*

In the town of Oposura,[15]
The bells began to ring,
And by the time I arrived,
The Zihuatanejo[16] had died.

At this point, the Black Poet says,

A plant called the holy thistle,
grows in the fields,
and if drought hadn't killed it
We'd be eating pork rinds now.

And this is when Old Man Vilmas says,

Crude and impish, New Mexico,
Filled with vassals, raised among goats,
Tell me, who has given you learning
In sufficient measure to crow among the gentry?

The Black Poet says,

Come out and joust if you are able,
And see if you might sing with clarity,
Like the lover who shows no fear,
But rather seeks the quest.

Open Samson's doors,
Along with those that grace your understanding,
And build that all may see,
The temple of the wise King Solomon.

King Solomon's temple
Is made of the wood of olive trees,

It has a glass door,
And a mirror at its threshold.

Old Man Vilmas says,

Sir, if you have wit and reason,
I ask you,
Tell us, where lies the grave,
Where Adam was buried?

And the Black Poet says,

Adam was buried in Africa, in a place no one would
    suspect,
In a field fit for hiding things,
In a cave, hear me well,
Which I can confirm,
Was on the road to Jerusalem.

If you hear and understand me,
And your memory is sound,
Pray, tell me what happened to
The thirty dinars[17] for which
Christ was sold and betrayed?

Old Man Vilmas says,

Those thirty dinars
Where used to buy some land,

Where passing pilgrims
Could be buried,
when they died.

Old Man Vilmas says,

Pray tell, you who knows all things,
If you dare to say,
Which fault is as light as a feather,
And yet, leads to the biggest sin?
Speak, and let the questioning come to an end.

Old Man Vilmas says,

Listen to my voice as if it be from on high.
The gravest sin is to chime,
Like a clock and while away the time,
For whoever does not respect his parents,
Does not respect God Almighty.

So, at God's tribunal
Who will be condemned?
The one who is paid to sin,
Or the one who pays for having sinned?

That's when the Black Poet says,

I innocently ask,
That you please widen my understanding,

And explain this matter,
In a way that opens the mind.

Hear me, oh laudable and wise teacher,
Now, your nicely rendered song,
Strikes me as admirable,
And demonstrates your sharp wit.

That's when the Black Poet says,

Hear me, most lauded and wise teacher,
Oh, learned and schooled philosopher.
Build up my budding talent,
And steady my wobbly judgment.

You, so wise and learned,
So sure of your keen science.
I ask, by your reasoning,
What idea is first to rhyme?

All that I know and hold in mind,
Must proclaim the truth,
Look, the first is faith,
Then hope, and then comes charity.

He [the Black Poet] says,

Which Christ should we value more?
Christ crucified on the cross

or Christ, the Lord
Who at the Last Supper
Shared his body to nourish Man?
Pray tell, if your wit is so sharp?

He [Old Man Vilmas] says,

And this reply I repeat,
God appears to Man
At the table of the Altar,
This when on the day of one's
Penance and repentance,
One goes up to receive communion.

The Black Poet, again, inquires,

I shall ask of your wisdom, a second time,
From your considerable knowledge,
Tell me, which is the grandest bird
To grace the court of heaven?

Old Man Vilmas says,

I'll give you that answer,
Pure as the poetry you wield,
In the court of heaven,
Ave Mary[18] is the one name
Uttered at every hour of the day and night.

Old Man Vilmas says,

If you know your philosophy,
And your mind is razor sharp,
What was it my good God wished to do
and was not able to?

The Black Poet says,

Up there in God's heavens,
The Lord God declares,
he can't make up lies
As big as those the two of us tell.

[Old Man Vilmas]

God made this world,
This being, his first supreme deed,
Now, tell me how as firstborn,
Your father managed to keep you in the fold?

The Black Poet says,

In the full benefit of your knowing,
If you know anything at all about aristocracy
It was by original sin,
Tempered with the spirit of grace.
That Mary bore Jesus
And God formed Mary,

But you have yet to explain,
What debt this incurred?

Here the Black Poet says,

What debt was incurred you ask?
As he came from heaven to earth
Given that he was a God of life
And he descended from heaven
To reign on earth.

Listen, you bigmouthed flowerpot,
listen, wordy old man,
I ask, who stayed in the heavens
When God became man?

[Old Man Vilmas]

I'll supply you an answer,
Given its grave importance,
God the Son became incarnate,
While up in heaven God the Father remains,
To judge us all.

There, that's as much as I recall of that trova.
Now, concerning Gracia Istavera[19] *and Old Man Vilmas.*
It starts out,

[Gracia]

Maestro Vilmas, just where have you been?
Lo these many days and weeks?
How we have searched high and low for you
Sending companies of
Pony soldiers to find you.

[Old Man Vilmas]

My, but your powers are nil,
Now that I report to you here,
And ask, just where are all the legions
that have gone to search for me,
Lo these many days and weeks,
And have not managed to find me?

Today, I have you in my crosshairs,
I shall judge how to improvise your verses.
I've heard that you are Gracia,
But I say don't mess with me.

[Gracia]

All the Graces[20] I'd say, if it were left to me,
And you'd quickly fall from grace,
Maestro, you'd do well to aim with care,
and keep an eye on these verses,
think, while you try to keep up

23

And though you'd like to fly
your old age keeps you bound to earth.

Old Man Vilmas says,

No one complains on hearing my voice
And in all arenas, I am victorious,
Though I may speak of lofty or common things,
Vain things or things full of mirth,
Just imagine, the scandal that would fall on this old man,
Should a pipsqueak like you win out.

Then Gracia tells him,

I'm Sir Grace,
Known to sing by day and by night,
But, Maestro, please deliver in song,
Your treatise on philosophy.

Old Man Vilmas says,

In the name of Mary, most holy,
I'll write you a new story,
If you are fit to know philosophy,
To let your voice fly,
For heaven's sake!
What thing did God first make?
Where is the river of glass?
Where did Mary walk on the earth?

Where in the constellations is the eastern star?
And what name is given
To the most important garden?

Would-be songwriters and part-time poets,
Let me now inquire of you,
What colors did He give the heavens?
Before his notable death
And before he made the heavens
What things did God leave undone?

Then Gracia says,

Maestro, do you really want to hear my song?
In this I am most befuddled,
For how could you ask me to divine
Such exceedingly lofty matters?

Old Man Vilmas speaks,

Here we go, and all should pay attention,
Little bard, know your place,
To what use have you put your schooling?
Hear me, celebrated Gracia,
It's your own sin of pride
That brings you to my sight
For all can see your impotence,
Still, may your verses steady you,

As you face this old man
Who's about to crush your efforts.

From my knowledge of philosophy,
Before he made the heavens,
He made the light of day.
So, there you have it, idle gossips,
Don't place your faith in night owls,
Tavera is just about to make his point,
And take your pulse.

Who would dare to amble through
The palace of the King?
For those who don't know me,
I should say my verses end here
And send forth the news
That this is where Tavera
Matched Old Man Vilmas.

This is as much as I know of this one. Okay, I'll recite one more song, a décima *called "The* Décima *of the Kings." Now, pay attention to what the foundation of the first strophe is. Since each verse needs to link back to the first strophe. Here it goes:*

The Décima of the Kings

Cry, cry, dear heart, cry,
Cry if you feel betrayed,

There is no shame
In a man crying for a woman.

The wise Solomon[21] wept
For an unfaithful princess,
Jacob cried for Rachel,[22]
And Samson pleaded for his life.

As he entered a great hall,
He wept for Adriana's[23] immense cruelty,
Appealing to her sense of loyalty,
Though by this time he had lost her affections,
And so with all your might,
Cry, dear heart, cry.

The Greek cried for Helena,[24]
Dismas[25] bit his lips,
Even Caesar, who ruled as Octavius,
Wept then for Helena.

David lamented his troubles,
And thought of Bathsheba,[26]
David wept for his son Chileab,[27]
When he was kidnapped.

And if he is now despised,
He weeps for his love, why?

Pharez wept for Tamar[28]
As Ahasuerus wept for Esther.[29]

Pharaoh scorned the pleasure
That King Balthasar[30] enjoyed,
And Alexander[31] learned to weep,
For the magnificence of Troy.

Nothing of this is surprising,
Not I alone affirm,
That men must cry,
Cry, lonely heart, cry,
There's no shame
In a man crying for a woman.

Diocletian[32] spent days weeping in the forest,
After seeing a drawing of his beloved,
And Charlemagne[33] wept like a child,
And he was a mighty sovereign.

Freire[34] the churchman wept,
This I say and this I understand,
Tender hearts, cry onto the heavens,
For even Kings are known
To break down and weep for a woman.

This is where I close, with the foundational verse:

Cry, dear heart, cry
There is no shame
In a man crying for a woman.

Well, that song comes, well, I learned it from my father. And from what I know about the reply, he learned it from a man name Juan José Durán, who was headed to Chapelle, New Mexico. He was kind to him. He would always pull him aside and say, "Sit here, young man, under this cypress tree." And that's where he learned it, and I learned the same from my father.

4. "The Ballad of a Buffalo Hunter," from the oral tradition

As sung to the translator by Cleofes Vigil,
30 April 1986, Salt Lake City, Utah

Mister Cleofes Vigil shared his repertoire of New Mexico music, including this ballad, during a personal interview with the translator in Salt Lake City in 1986. In his recitation, Vigil, a well-known musician and folk artist, employs five- and six-line stanzas with verses of eight syllables held together by consonantal rhyme.

Vigil follows the classic form of the Spanish *décima*, which consists of ten-verse strophes of octosyllabic lines with a consonantal rhyming scheme. Vigil's ballad is a story-poem that conveys the details of the tragic death of Juan de Dios Maés, who is accidentally killed on a buffalo hunt to the Llano Estacado, the great plains of West Texas. These expanses of prairie land are proximate to the interior of New Mexico and were routinely visited by Nuevomexicano stockmen and ranchers to hunt buffalo as a way to supplement the needs of their home villages. When sung, the poem evokes the shared grief of the community as it learns of the untimely death of a young horseman and hunter who dies in the fullness of his life. Using death as a narrative vantage point, the verses are tailored to magnify the emotions of a community gripped by grief. The effect jolts listeners, who seem to hear the voice of the dead buffalo hunter announcing his premonition and acceptance of death as it comes to claim him. The expressive power of the ballad is comparable to that achieved by the legendary bluegrass master Ralph Stanley in his haunting rendition of the traditional Appalachian folk song "Oh, Death."

The balladeer does not throttle back notions of grief, mourning, or pathos but seeks every opportunity to make the ordinariness of life collide with the abruptness of its end. A resonant power is found in Maés's final farewell, or *despedida*, to kin and neighbors. Each succeeding verse becomes a lugubrious address to parents, friends, neighbors, relatives, and, finally, his wife, all of whom show up in the final stanza as the mourners accompanying the dead buffalo hunter to his final resting place. For more on the tradition of verse memorializing in New Mexico, see Meléndez.

Work Cited

Meléndez, A. Gabriel. "'Adios Acompañamiento': Text and Context of a New Mexican Alabado." *Chicano Discourse: Selected Conference Proceedings of the National Association for Chicano Studies*, edited by Tatcho Mindiola, Jr., and Emilio Zamora, U of Houston, Mexican American Studies Program, 1992, pp. 105–15.

The Ballad of a Buffalo Hunter

I found myself on the Colorado River
Biting into a watermelon,
Surrounded by my brothers,
Who kept great company.

Oh, my sorrel horse,
If I could ride you just once more
And ride you out as far as the buffalo hunt,
But even the best-laid plans
Often go astray!

Of those on the hunt,
my horse was the fastest,
But to my misfortune,
It stepped into a prairie dog hole,
My lance how it flew
How it pierced my body through!

Goodbye, my sorrel horse,
On you I rode with death,
I was so very tired,
That, the reins, I let drop
And you, my godmother Sebastiana,
Were there to set me free!

Goodbye, Lauriana Maés
And to that place at my front window,
Goodbye, to my mother, Donaciana,
And my father, Juan de Dios Maés,
Ay, ay, ay, ay.

When word of this gets back
All across New Mexico,
Many will grieve, no doubt,
The death of a *cibolero*
Ay, ay, ay, ay.

Goodbye, my sweet, young bride,
Goodbye, Romancita Maés,
Like a nopal that bears no fruit,
A widow you shall remain.
Ay, ay, ay, ay.

Now, I lie out somewhere out on the plains,
Like seed strewn to the wind
On the banks of that peaceful lake
Where my friends buried me
Ay, ay, ay, ay.

They have lifted my body
And have mounted their swift horses,
To recall where my body is buried

Down by the Colorado River.[35]

Ay, ay, ay, ay.

To sing this story in an Indian way,

One needs voice and grace,

To sing it so it shines

Like a well-polished gem

Just the way García sang it

In the plaza at Taos[36] one day

Ay, ay, ay, ay.

5. "Yikes! The Train Is Coming," Jesús María Hilario Alarid

El Independiente, vol. 2, no. 15, 29 June 1895,
Las Vegas, New Mexico

Jesús María Hilario Alarid (1834–1917) developed oratori-
cal and verbal skills that were nurtured in the oral tradi-
tions of his community. In time, the titles of *bardo* ("bard")
and *maestro* ("teacher") would be conferred upon him by
neighbors and friends. In village society these titles were
reserved for the most respected individuals in the commu-
nity. At Galisteo, New Mexico, a village thirty miles south
of Santa Fe, Alarid taught reading and writing in the lower
grades and served as an intermediary between village so-
ciety and the outside world. He also founded a musical
troupe that was frequently asked to provide entertainment
at secular and religious gatherings across northern New
Mexico and southern Colorado. His poetry and writings
begin to appear in Spanish-language newspapers in the late

1880s and reveal him to be a man of above-average intelligence. His command of composition and the verbal arts came from his formal study in private schools and equally so from oral performative skills rooted in traditional Nuevomexicano poetics.

In 1895 Alarid chose to entertain the readers of *El Independiente* (*The Independent*), a newspaper based in Las Vegas, New Mexico, with a jovial and humorous sketch in verse of a friend whose habit had become to call out in a loud voice, "¡Viene el ferrocarril!" ("The train is coming!"). The poem takes the form of a *cuarteto* (quatrain), a four-line stanza of eight-syllable verses in consonantal rhyme. Alarid's verses comment on the conundrum of change that figured in the rapid modernization of New Mexico. In this case that change is most apparent in the arrival of the railroad and its impact on what had been an isolated network of rural villages and ranches. Despite the fatal consequence of his friend being crushed by a locomotive, the event is treated with irony and humor. Unlike funerary oratory or elegy in verse, the deceased is not named, as would have been required by funerary etiquette, nor are his virtues and attributes enumerated for all to grieve. Indeed, the details of this death are so nebulous that the case is rendered as if it were imagined or hypothetical. It's possible that Alarid is not representing a real fatality or the loss of a neighbor but rather is ironizing a situation facing all Nuevomexicanos as they confront the arrival of a locomotive, actual or symbolic, that threatens to run them down. For more on Alarid's role in Nuevomexicano letters, see Meléndez 34–42.

Work Cited

Meléndez, A. Gabriel. *So All Is Not Lost: The Poetics of Print in Nuevomexicano Communities, 1834–1958*. U of New Mexico P, 1997.

Yikes! The Train Is Coming

Yikes! The train is coming,
These verses he liked to sing.
But who'd be keen enough to know,
That it was about to kill him?

I went to his house on one occasion,
There, puffed up with satisfaction,
He conjured disputes with me,
That brought him great joy.

And as often happens,
He kept on ribbing me
With joy and pleasure
With his wife by his side.

And he'd sing with gusto,
Yikes! The train is coming,
Putting on a great show
of pure pleasure,
Laughter and delight.

All day and all night,
It was a feast like no other,
With no thought in mind
that later things would sour,
and turn to pain and sadness.

Such tragedy, such sorrow
When least he expected it,
And to continue with the tale
These verses he would sing.

I lament your sad demise,
I shall not soon forget you,
Knowing that this bond of friendship
Will hold between us for eternity.

This bond will never be broken,
And will last even beyond death,
But who'd be keen enough to know,
Would dare to imagine,
That a train was about to kill him
Goodbye, my dear friend,
Farewell, my loyal friend,
You've always been held in high regard,
Ever guarding the bond of our friendship.

And now you've gone to rest
Up to the heavenly mansion.
But who could have anticipated,
And such a crazy thing have imagined.

That one sad and fateful day,
That a train would come and kill him.

6. "Some of Chicoria's Verses: The Best-Known Poet among the Oldest Residents of New Mexico," Camilo Padilla (editor)

La Revista Ilustrada, vol. 12, no. 10,
June 1925, El Paso, Texas

As editor of *La Revista Ilustrada* (*The Illustrated Review*), Camilo Padilla gave space in his publication to items submitted by his subscribers. He especially welcomed items concerning Nuevomexicano customs, arts, and literary culture. One such item appearing in 1925 features verses attributed to the legendary troubadour known as "Chicoria."[37] The submission from Felipe Márquez, a resident of the village of San Mateo, in western New Mexico, obviously delighted Padilla, since it provided a way to showcase the feats of the legendary Chicoria, who Padilla lauds as "un gran poeta de clase humilde" ("a great poet of the poor classes"). The verses are prefaced by details of the life of this renowned poet and of his importance to the continuation of the community's expressive culture.

The submission further provides a means of understanding how the *trova* tradition was transmitted over time from one generation to the next. Padilla remarks on how valued and ubiquitous the *trovas* once were and how, regrettably, they were fading from use. Márquez's submission establishes a living link to the days of the famed troubadours. Like many other villagers, Márquez learned of Chicoria in his youth and performed his compositions when the occasion permitted. For more on Padilla and the significant cultural work he carried out in journalism and through his publication of *La Revista Ilustrada,* see Meléndez 69–72, 195–201.

Work Cited

Meléndez, A. Gabriel. *So All Is Not Lost: The Poetics of Print in Nuevomexicano Communities, 1834–1958*. U of New Mexico P, 1997.

Some of Chicoria's Verses

We bring to publication the verses of a great poet of the poor classes, who became known for his fluid improvisations throughout the state of New Mexico, and who everyone lovingly referred to as "the poet Chicoria."

These verses were improvised by our poet at a banquet given by some rich people, to which no poor person was admitted. Chicoria was the only one allowed to attend so that he could delight the group as the gathering went on.

The couplets and the information we have about them were supplied to us by our friend and collaborator Mister Felipe Márquez of San Mateo, New Mexico, a person who also is inspired to write verses once in a while—and some are very good, indeed.

Readers in New Mexico will surely appreciate that we have published the verses, since we have wanted to remind them of the festive mind of this bard who was loved for over two generations, and with this we want to show that we continue with our efforts to obtain more compositions by Chicoria and by the Black Poet.[38]

Taking everything into account,
My, but what a stain on life is poverty!
It doesn't resemble anything
that those with wealth enjoy,
It's clear that folks with money,
Get seated at the head of the table.

They go about with such conceit,
No matter what might happen,
While today you might be well-fed.
And tomorrow face starvation,
And this happens often,
As time comes and goes.

Nothing in this life endures,
Good things, bad things,
all come to an end,
And we are all leveled to the same fate,
By a same, sad burial plot,
The same is true for beasts of the fields,
Whose destiny is also death.

People with money exude wealth,
And enjoy nothing but the best,
But a person who has nothing,
Exudes nothing and leaves not a trace,

And when he leaves to work at dawn
He must even leave his loved ones behind.

It doesn't help to be young or single,
No edge is given to the well-respected man,
Only money has worth,
Doesn't matter whose,
But with it
Everything will go your way.

I'm just one of Adam's children.
Born before my time,
Here I shall improvise a saying,
Even if some think me crass,
I'll end up with something to eat today,
if any leftovers remain,
Since you all know I'm of no concern to anyone.

God thought well of poverty,
But since he didn't know how it was lived,
Until he came to earth,
And saw, firsthand, how fierce a force it is,
He bolted and ran,
Not stopping until he was standing
before the gates of heaven.

7. "An Original New Mexican Story: Poor Emilio!," Camilo Padilla

La Gaceta de Mora, vol. 1, no. 27,
14 August 1890, Mora, New Mexico

A native of Santa Fe, New Mexico, Camilo Padilla (1864–
1933), who wrote under the pen name "Zulu," was active in the Spanish-language newspaper movement that crested in the 1890s. He was among the most respected members of the Hispanic-American Press Association, the first professional association of Spanish-language editors and journalists in the Southwest. A seasoned traveler, Padilla had the opportunity to live in Washington, DC, where he worked as the private secretary to Antonio Joseph, New Mexico's territorial delegate. While in Washington, Padilla continued to collaborate with newspapers in New Mexico and frequently sent them communiqués in the form of editorial opinions, travel narratives, and other topics of cross-cultural interest. These items, meant for a local readership, are some of the earliest writings from a Nuevomexicano perspective that examine social and cultural boundaries, made readily visible to Padilla through his sojourns to the East Coast. "¡Pobre Emilio!" ("Poor Emilio!"), a short story set in Washington, DC, tells of a young man, a close friend of the narrator's, who has the opportunity to work in the nation's capital. While living in the city, Emilio falls in love with an Anglo woman. The story relates how differences in language, culture, and religion make the relationship impossible. A dramatic moment in the story comes when a distraught Emilio attempts to take his own life. Just as he is about to place a revolver to his head, Emilio has a vision that provides him with a reason to live and convinces him to dedicate himself to the defense of his people and homeland.

As a journalist, poet, and essayist, Padilla was a constant force in promoting Nuevomexicano print culture. He is among the first of his generation to explore how fiction and creative storytelling might serve to illuminate social and political concerns impinging on questions of identity, attachment to a homeland, and the cultural values of Nuevomexicanos as a distinct population in the United States. For more on Padilla, see Meléndez 69–72, 154–58.

Work Cited

Meléndez, A. Gabriel. *So All Is Not Lost: The Poetics of Print in Nuevomexicano Communities, 1834–1958*. U of New Mexico P, 1997.

An Original New Mexican Story: Poor Emilio!

It had been four years since a young friend left New Mexico to go to the East Coast.

While we waited at the train station in the old historic city of Santa Fe, I don't know for what reason I began to think that such a trip would not turn out to be a happy one, nor would it be as my friend had dreamt it might be. I begged him not to leave. My pleading was in vain. That night he left the city that had been his cradle amid a symphony of military music from a band that was at the station for the arrival of the gallant but unfortunate patriot John A. Logan.[39] As the train was departing with my childhood friend on board, my eyes filled with tears as I watched it leave. I felt my heart break, and a premonition came to me that I would never again see my good friend Emilio, this patriot that my homeland was losing this night.

Emilio was a young man of around twenty-five years old. He was of humble parents who nonetheless had provided him with a good education. He not only excelled in his studies but was blessed with brilliant talent. His last two years at school were so superb that his teachers recognized his potential, and they envisioned a very happy and bright future for him. He had such a pleasant personality and was well-liked by everyone that he encountered. He was as meek as a poet. His only weakness was that he fell hard for women.

Two years after Emilio left, some accident of fate caused me to visit the city in the East where Emilio was living, which was none other than the nation's capital. It was a magnificent city. Emilio was waiting for me at the train station, and the joy he experienced when he saw me was indescribable. His round face was glowing with that most beautiful light, that of friendship. He hugged me and said to me, "Oh, God, my friend, man am I happy to see you!"

I got a room next to Emilio's. We were able to get together every night to chat and go for a walk. What memorable times those were! We had been chatting about New Mexico and the people of New Mexico and about the beauty of the city and its attractions. Oh, such precious and blessed conversations we had, and which now seem like the flight of mindless birds never to return again. As we talked, my friend's beautiful dark eyes would fill with tears. I recall a particular episode of his life, which I will now narrate.

The year after I came to visit him in that city, I learned that another friend had introduced him to a young seventeen-year-old girl. As it turned out, she was as cruel as she was lovely, but all that needed to happen for my friend to fall in love with her was for him to see her once. Emilio continued to see her, and every day his love for her grew. It appeared as if she, too, might reciprocate.

One night after having returned from a walk, Emilio, in very tender words, confessed to Miss X that he loved her with all his heart. Upon hearing this, the young girl began to cry. When my friend asked if she loved him in return, she did not answer and only kept crying. Emilio persisted so much that she finally said that she did love him but that she felt conflicted and burdened by a problem that would not permit them to be married in a church. She said to him, "You are a Catholic and I am a Presbyterian. It is as impossible for me to change my religion as it is for you." He had been so infatuated with her that he had not paid attention[40] to this matter. When he heard the words she spoke fall from her lips, he felt as though he had been struck by a bolt of lightning. Yet he was so deeply in love with her that he regained his composure and replied, "If you promise to love me, I will give up my religion, my

44

family, my honor, and my entire future for you." And so, I ask you to love me as I love you." Alas, a drastic change of heart had come to this young lady. Lacking the noble sentiments that characterize Latin women, she heartlessly said to him, "The truth is that I don't love you."

Emilio was stunned and remained so for a time after hearing these words. When he regained his senses, he still did not know what to do. Should he leave that place and that cruel woman, or should he kill her and kill himself right then and there? Oh, dear readers, how often do thoughts like these overtake the mind of a young lover? In the end, God intervened and granted Emilio prudence and good judgment at that critical moment, and he left the home of that heartless Yankee[41] lady. Emilio went to his room to try to get some sleep, but sleep eluded him that night. When he finally did drift off to sleep, his dreams raged with storms and nightmarish scenes.

From that night on, traces of deep pain became visible on his forehead. His eyes lost the seductive brilliance that had so characterized Emilio. His face now bore resemblance to Heinrich Heine.[42] This young man—a young man who had never been easily overwhelmed by life's countless storms, who had always forged ahead on his own, and who, had it not been for this incident, was destined to occupy the most distinguished positions in his hometown—now found himself so sad and dejected that he could not manage to raise his eyes even to speak to a friend. He often would say to me, "Nowhere in the world are there women as passionate, tender, and sincere as are our women—Mexican women. By comparison, 'our little cousins' are quite the opposite. They are cold, materialistic, conniving, and manipulative. Mexican women, such noble women, God bless them, a thousand times over!" When he'd finished saying this, he would insist that was how he truly felt and would shed a tear.

It was clear that he still loved the object of his torment such that he visited her and forgave her. Strangely, he took the view that he would grow in his love and suffering for her in a way that recalls the early Christian martyrs who, when put to death and enveloped by flames, are seen smiling and shining in the flames. And yet, that merciless Yankee girl remained as cold as a statue and treated him with greater contempt as each day passed. The purest and noblest love is always the most fortunate, but like a ship that does not find a port it remains adrift.

In time Emilio nearly forgot about the young Miss X, but at times, like a bitter drink, the thought of taking his own life returned to him. In these moments, he would get over his troubles as few other men could, and the kindness he was known for would shine through. So few are the men that can do this that they compel our admiration. One day he took a revolver and was going to shoot himself when a dark cloud appeared before him, and there he saw two images that were very dear to him. In one he saw his mother, and in the other he saw his homeland. At that moment he put down the pistol on a table and fell to his knees weeping and said, "If it were not for you, my dear mother, and my homeland, I would blow my brains out! But, perhaps, you have need of my humble service, and so I will hide my suffering behind a fake smile, and I shall defend you with my voice, pen, and sword. I am wedded to you, beloved homeland, and I live only for you until the day you have no further need of my service, and then I shall fade away. In the meantime, I will bear my pain and carry my chains. May God bless all those who have shown me kindness, those who are so noble, so beautiful, so magnificent!"

Two years later, I came to be in the nation's capital. There I received a telegram from Cuba. The telegram was from a close friend who had sailed with Emilio to Cuba. He informed me that the ship on which they sailed from New York to Cuba had sunk near the island and that Emilio was among those aboard who had perished. It took effort to restrain myself from doing something foolish, so far was I from my homeland, the homeland of this young patriot, Emilio.

Today is the twenty-seventh of June, exactly a year to the day of receiving that fateful telegram informing me of the death of my closest friend. And now, I bring to publication this chapter in the life of this young man filled with inspiring patriotism. I do this as a way to honor his noble actions, and I ask you, dear reader, to mourn his death with me.

8. "The Fandango," José Rómulo Ribera

El Boletín Popular, vol. 11, no. 17,
6 February 1896, Santa Fe, New Mexico

José Rómulo Ribera (1848–1917) was among a small group of young men in New Mexico who were recruited to the priesthood by the archbishop of Santa Fe, Jean Baptiste Lamy, newly installed in 1850. Ribera's training as a seminarian informed his craft as a writer and poet. By the time he submitted "El fandango" ("The Fandago") to *El Boletín Popular* (*The Popular Bulletin*), a Santa Fe weekly, Ribera had left the priesthood and was engaged as a merchant in Wallace, New Mexico, where he lived with his wife and children.

Three features of Ribera's work distinguish his writings: his erudite stance, his work as a popular poet, and his work as a commissioned or solicited poet. "The Fandango" reflects Ribera's cultivation of popular and satirical verses. Ribera employs the popular and the sturdy mold of *cuartetos* (quatrains), four eight-syllable verses with consonantal rhyme (*abab, abba*). These verses in the *arte menor*, or vernacular, tradition present a gaudy, festive, and exuberant description of one of the weekly fandangos customarily held in towns large and small in New Mexico.

Ribera offers an insider's view of a pastime that had become an object of curious speculation and often of derision for Americans who had recently arrived in New Mexico from the East. Of the fandango, W. W. H. Davis noted, "In New Mexico the general name of all assemblies where dancing is the principal amusement is *fandango*. Every class and rank in society participates in the amusement and very small children are seen whirling in the waltz and tripping in the dance with the same gusto as their more mature companions" (315). Dancing in general garnered the suspicion of Anglo-Protestants, but even for Nuevomexicanos, the fascination with fandangos had to do with how the event suspended notions of comportment associated with ordinary and mundane life and made visible the irregular and unpredictable behavior associated with festive and bacchanal pleasures.

While Anglo-Americans might not have been aware, fandangos were highly regulated affairs. For example, they could not be staged during Lent. Alcohol could not be served on location, and a dance captain, or *bastonero*, kept order by signaling the start and end of the fandango and watching over the comportment of dance partners. Men were bound by rules of honor to seek the consent of female dance partners and could not break social mores by selecting an ineligible dance partner (a married woman, for example). Still, the clandestine use of alcohol could upset all decorum. On occasion, as happens in Ribera's poem, a *bastonero* could lose control to rowdies in attendance.

Ribera caricatures the guests in attendance at his fandango by taking aim, in a good-natured way, at the exaggerated opinions they hold of themselves. Their pretenses are ripe for mocking and trigger laughter in other guests. For more on Ribera's contributions to the Spanish-language press in New Mexico and the more erudite features of his work, see Meléndez 158–62. Davis's *El Gringo* details the author's views of the mores and customs of the Nuevomexicanos (160–322).

Works Cited

Davis, W. W. H. *El Gringo: New Mexico and Her People*. 1857. Reprint ed., U of Nebraska P, 1982.

Meléndez, A. Gabriel. *So All Is Not Lost: The Poetics of Print in Nuevomexicano Communities, 1834–1958*. U of New Mexico P, 1997.

The Fandango

Mister Valeriano got hitched,
Fame surrounded the wedding,
The people, every last person,
Stood in line to shake his hand.

Let them make a happy couple, God willing,
Give them a long and happy life.
She is lovely and unpretentious,
And there's no wild streak in her.

She's a wee bit tall, thin as a rail,
Dark-skinned and beautiful eyes
She dons a hefty pair of spectacles,
She's not fat and she is not slim.

She doesn't have lofty ambitions,
She does like to show off her boots,
But she knows how to mend underwear,
and sew up holes in socks.

She's something of an early riser,
A hard-working woman, well-behaved,
By sunrise she's about,
Having had her breakfast.

That said, everyone is now dancing,
Let's look in on them, shall we?
With all the people in attendance
Surely, we'll come away with some gossip.

Making the rounds is Lady Juana,
Very dolled up and bewitching
There, too, strolls Lady Teodora
Followed by Lady Feliciana.

Joaquín's daughter
Looking like a poppy flower
And oh, dear, Lola, too,
Is looking like a jasmine's flower.

Another young lady kept smiling.
As she is asked to dance,
She is blind in one eye
And can't see much with the other.

It's great to know that pure joy
Like a ruling queen

Ruled all the livelong day
Only to die out at dawn.

Canes pounded the dance floor
And Luis, the dance leader, arrived
And with him entered a quarrelsome fellow,
Who happened to be missing an arm.

The fellow rose to dance without
Sir Luis's permission
And, ready or not,
Sir Luis shoved him off the dance floor.

The fellow was greatly offended,
And was feeling sorely disrespected,
He called Luis a bigheaded fool
And said he reminded him of the Cyclops Polyphemus.[43]

Feeling like his authority was eroding,
Sir Luis without much thought
Got up from his seat,
And without warning,

Lunged at the dizzy man,
With unexpected brutishness
And had he not chased him out,
He might have lost his life.

Great was the ruckus,
And great the commotion,
From a fair distance away,
the groom sadly observed his bride,
Sitting helpless and alone.

He had good reason to fear
That the beleaguered bride
Would call out to him for help,
As she began to faint in the corner of the hall.

Many people went over to gingerly pick up
Poor Secundina.
They dragged and hauled her
Leaving her to wait
in the kitchen.

There she was hugged and made safe,
From the insults and the shouting
Then they sprinkled her with holy water,
And rushed her away to the balcony.

And from there it was best to observe
The unbelievable scene
Of a crowd ready to fight
Of common folk snorting and shouting.

The dance hall emptied out,
Cobwebs dangled from above.
Guys and gals were decked out on the floor
As the sun of a new day began to rise.

All told, five guests lay wounded,
Six had busted heads,
Everyone was bent and bruised,
And some were barely standing.

It came to pass that
Secundina was released from prison,
And three times in a row she swore that
"Prison has the best cafeteria."

Oh, these dances and these big parties,
Leave sad memories in their wake,
But today folks are singing,
And are asking in their morning prayers,
"Peace here below, as later we'll be in glory."

III. New Mexico:
Not New, Not Mexico

9. "Dark Nights in San Miguel County" (excerpts), Manuel Cabeza de Baca

El Sol de Mayo, vol. 1, no. 43, 18 February 1892,
Las Vegas, New Mexico (parts 1–2)

El Sol de Mayo, vol. 1, no. 44, 25 February 1892,
Las Vegas, New Mexico (parts 3–4)

The journalistic career of Manuel Cabeza de Baca (1853–1915) was framed by his career as an attorney and prosecutor. In an age when the order of pre-American days began to give way to factionalism and divisive politics, he saw his role as a guardian of an older and, to his mind, less violent time in New Mexico. In his own newspaper, *El Sol de Mayo* (*The May Sun*), Cabeza de Baca often took up subjects he encountered in his public charge as a prosecutor for San Miguel County.

When the railroad reached New Mexico in 1879, it ended the region's isolation and brought hundreds of Anglo-American settlers to north-central New Mexico. The *Gorras Blancas*, or White Caps, the subject of Cabeza de Baca's novella, were for the most part heirs to land grants who began to see their rights to land and water—established under a system of Spanish and Mexican land grants and preserved, in theory if not in practice, by the Treaty of Guadalupe Hidalgo—being usurped by Anglo-American land speculators and political cliques seeking control of the Las Vegas Land Grant in particular. While the *Gorras Blancas* were for the most part a paramilitary group, their founding members were originally associated with the Knights of Labor, a national labor movement and likely the group that provided the New Mexico organization with its distinctive white caps, which gave the organization its name.

Cabeza de Baca, whose life and actions were based on moral rectitude and personal character, had little sympathy for the extralegal methods espoused by the *Gorras Blancas*. Between February and March of 1892, Cabeza de Baca published his nine-part novella in *El Sol de Mayo* as a narrative indictment of the *Gorras Blancas* and of the labor leader and land grant activist Juan José Herrera. Herrera came to be called *El Gran Capitán*, or "The Great Captain." Cabeza de Baca considered the *Gorras Blancas* to be agents of terror and intimidation who were sowing hate and retribution amid the peaceful, law-abiding citizens of San Miguel County. To substantiate his claim, he includes the actual manifesto of the night riders, which appeared as a broadside pasted in the town plaza on a dark night in the 1890s. The novella quickly came to the attention of the Spanish-speaking readership of other leading newspapers and was hailed as an important literary work by other journalists. Writing in 1896, the poet and journalist José Escobar summed up Cabeza de Baca's promise as a writer, saying:

> [E]l libro del Sr. Lic. Baca, es una obra que pasará a la posteridad, sirviendo de mucho a los criminalistas y a los que sigan en la ímprova tarea de hacer la diseción fisiológica del corazón. Entre tanto, reciba el Lic. Baca nuestras más calurosas y justas felicitaciones por ese trabajo literario de verdadera utilidad social, y ojalá que su ejemplo estimule a la juventud nativa para que con hechos de ese género, podamos desvanecer los injustos cargos y torpes calumnias de los *touristas* que sin conocernos más que *a vuela tren*, nos acusan de falta de cultura y escasez absoluta de talento.

> Attorney Baca's book is a work that will pass into posterity and will be of great service to criminologists and those who face the laborious task that comes from dissecting the structures of the heart. For now,

we send our warmest and best congratulations to Attorney Baca for this work of literature that is a social good, and we hope that his example will push our native youth so that by producing works of this genre we may be able to fend off the unjust charges and the twisted lies of those *tourists* who only know us *as their trains race by,* those who accuse us of a lack of culture and of a total absence of talent.   (my trans.)

For more on the life and career of Cabeza de Baca, see Meléndez, *So All Is Not Lost* 77–81. For more on the activities of the *Gorras Blancas*, see Rosenbaum. For the details of Escobar's early assessment of the progress of letters in New Mexico, see Meléndez, "Certifiable Past."

Works Cited

Escobar, José. "Progreso literario de Nuevo México, sus periódicos, historiadores, sus poetas y novelistas." *Las Dos Repúblicas*, vol. 1, no. 27, 11 July 1896, p. 1.

Meléndez, A. Gabriel. "A Certifiable Past and the Possible Future of a Borderlands Literary and Cultural Episteme." *Writing/Righting History: Twenty-Five Years of Recovering the US Hispanic Literary Heritage*, edited by Antonia Castañeda and Clara Lomas, Arte Público Press, 2019, pp. 301–21.

———. *So All Is Not Lost: The Poetics of Print in Nuevomexicano Communities, 1834–1958.* U of New Mexico P, 1997.

Rosenbaum, Robert J. *Mexican Resistance in the Southwest: "The Sacred Right of Self-Preservation."* U of Texas P, 1981.

Dark Nights in San Miguel County

The illustration or graphic that heads up this history exactly represents the true likeness of the White Caps seen in full uniform and in the manner and form in which they have many times ridden through the streets of the villages and towns of San Miguel County and in the manner they will ride through other counties in the territory if peaceful people do nothing to prepare themselves to stop them and prevent them from continuing their infernal skirmishes.

There goes this militia from hell, recruited and enlisted by the Antichrist, who has in mind to reap a big harvest of fruits and labor resulting from the actions of the White Caps in San Miguel County.

Much has been written and said about this secret society of anarchists—much of this is well-known throughout the New Mexico territory and the United States as well—and about how, at one time, these night riders stirred up so much fear and terror. The actions of these rapacious night birds have repeatedly, by the stomping of their horses and the blasts of their guns, put in great danger the lives of the quiet and peaceful families and the citizenry of the county, and we will tell more about this true history, which we propose to write to give our readers an idea of the illegal acts committed by the White Caps and of their origins and why the group was organized.

1.

Night had fallen on 28 April 1889, and with it a rainstorm comparable to the first of the forty said to have fallen during the universal flood.[44] The storm grew into a pouring rain of thick droplets pushed along by a furious windstorm that formed a thick, foggy cloud bank that made it impossible to see from one end to the other across the plaza of Las Vegas. Every so often a jagged bolt of lightning cut across the sky and was instantly followed by the crack of thunder that cleared the sky, leaving only the reverberation of an echo.

The intensity of the storm kept people off the streets. Only three human shapes could be detected amid the flashes of light. The three had, by chance it seems, come together, seeking shelter from the storm. They huddled under the porch of a house that had once been a parish church. The three were the Great Captain, a stranger, and the town barber. It looked as if they were preoccupied, engaged as they were in a very interesting conversation that consisted of the following exchange:

"Hello," said the Great Captain. "This is a good time to speak to you about a plan I have that is as dark as this night but that cannot but bring good results if we move on it. I so much want to explain it to you, but you must keep it in utmost confidence and be reserved about it."

The stranger was eager to hear the secret plan and said, "Good! The time is right, and you can speak to me in confidence."

"I have come up with a master plan that will greatly improve our lot. I've submitted the plan to Mr. Blake and some other gentlemen. They think my plan is so worthy that they stand ready, not merely to light the fuse but to back it up with any material support needed to execute its operations."

"But what plan? What are these actions you speak of? Explain yourself!" replied the barber.

"Very well, very well indeed!" replied the Great Captain. "I'll tell you everything. I have traveled to Colorado, Wyoming, Kansas, Utah, and other states. I have acquired much experience. I have many ideas, and I can suggest the means and design to carry out an endeavor that, while risky, will make us winners. I've read the history of the Russian nihilists, the Italian Mafia, the Indiana White Caps, the Chicago anarchists, and finally, the constitution of the Knights of Labor.[45]

"You all know I'm no fool. I can speak English, French, and some indigenous languages. All this will help us when it comes time and we need to explain our aims. I propose to come up with a soup mix that includes all these ingredients. We'll sweeten the soup for the people under the pretext of being Knights of Labor, since there's no better plan of inducement than setting up as Knights of Labor. The order of the Knights is universal. It's a balm and a panacea for the working class against capitalists. It's a group that protects the poor, their salaries, and their constitutional rights. This is brilliant, and so we explain to the people that their wages will go up, that their wood will be worth twice as much as it's worth today, that corn, wheat, oats, chili, garlic, garbanzos, horsebeans, peas, squash, and onions, freighted to market by laborers, will get the highest of prices. Once we have built this platform, we'll bring in the question of the land grants, an issue that is sure to inflame and preoccupy everyone."

"Bravo," said the stranger, "I like your proposal, and I'm betting big on it."

"Once we're organized," replied the Great Captain, "we'll declare a vicious war against the rich. We'll tell everyone that the poor shall seize the reins and control the government, and down with the owners! The plan is to ruin property, cut fences, rip out railroad ties, burn haystacks and train bridges, and, in all, to intimidate and to make promises."

"But just where will we begin to organize what I think should be called the Knights of Labor as a guise and cover for the White Caps, nihilists, Mafia, and anarchists?" the stranger asked.

"No place better for this," responded the Great Captain, "than the Plaza del Burro. It's an isolated location, far from everything. You won't even find snitches there. It's perfect for this pressing and urgent situation. We'll give Mrs. Crisanta some money so she can make some hoods and uniforms for us that will fully disguise our identity."

The barber appeared to be very confused and nervous. He sweated profusely, as if the downpour had landed only on him. He could not truly understand the real intent of this heartless man who without a conscience addressed them. And so, he kept silent but vigilant. He wanted to better understand how this monster could possibly carry out his plans. The barber felt his stomach turn as he listened to the crafty and cunning captain. He silently swore to all the saints in heaven that he would expose him at the first opportunity. At this point and without continuing the conversation, the three of them went their separate ways. The barber remained still for a time with his head down, still thinking about all he had heard from the mouth of a man he now considered a bandit. The terrifying confabulation seemed like a bad dream that he could not fully grasp, and yet, here was a fearful reality that threatened the destruction of San Miguel County and the property of its citizens. What troubled him the most was that a number of respectable people might succumb and lend support to this infernal project.

If carried out, the plot would bring down on the heads of the New Mexicans the worst kind of foul reputation and would brand them with the charge of barbarism and would confirm and serve to justify previous reports and hostile attitudes toward them. This barber was after all a real member of the Knights of Labor. He had belonged to the order for years in California and other places. In those places, the order had never loaned itself out or engaged in criminal acts. Yet he was willing to dig deeper and find a solution to the terrible dilemma he faced. He would go along with it, operating like an investigator, and learn all he could. Admittedly, he liked the idea of initiating some kind of political reform, though his conscience would not permit him to resort to improper and nefarious activities. He told himself, "Let's see where the ball lands."

Suddenly the heaving of a drunken policeman leaving a nearby tavern who was about to vomit and spill out his guts startled the barber and brought him back from these deep thoughts. He lifted his gaze and, looking upward, saw a magnificent spectacle. The night winds had all but cleared away the dark, tempestuous clouds, leaving behind a blue sky sprinkled with pale stars and the brilliant light of the moon as it appeared on the horizon. In the distance a large comet could be seen streaking across a pure and beautiful sky. The passing phenomena seemed to announce an era of misfortune and trouble for San Miguel County. This happenstance could not have been more coincidental.

2.

Readers are aware of the interesting conversation these three carried out on this stormy night along with the Great Captain's boundless ambitions. The day after that conversation, the great disrupter of the peace could be seen running from one place to the next, hopping like a cricket from village to village and making his way to every nook and cranny in the county. He convened gatherings and secret meetings, inciting citizens to enlist as soldiers in his new army. He painted a bright, happy future for them and false promises until he managed to form a group of fence-cutting mafiosos, nihilists, anarchists, and White Caps under the guise he had indicated in his conversations with the barber and the stranger. This is how the nocturnal procession had its early beginning. Once the misbegotten group was sworn to secrecy, members blindly vowed to their leaders that they would carry out their hellish activities. Three full years of calamities, detestable acts, misery, and errors are due to the Great Captain's master plan.

3.

The night of 2 November 1890 had something about it that marked it as unusual. It seemed an exceedingly long night, quiet and serene; time seemed to slow, waiting for the sun to dawn, and only the humming of the wind and a faint rustling of the trees was heard in the distance. The moon had not yet set, and all seemed to be in harmony. The residents of the town, except for the few night owls still up at the taverns, enjoyed the sweetness of a deep slumber. A few were still at the bars and taverns hoping sleep would overtake them so they, too, could retire to the same sweet slumber of their neighbors. Some of the town policemen fell in with the barroom patrons and tried their hand at gambling. Some played poker, and others hoped to win at the billiard tables. Everything was completely submerged in silence on this night of perfect tranquility.

Suddenly, at twelve midnight, a troop of sixty White Caps (in the uniform of their fence-cutting actions) rode into town along the street leading to the bridge. They entered slowly and with deadly silence. Only the whistle issued by their leaders and the hoofbeats of their horses sounded out. As they went along, they dispersed some anonymous leaflets. An exact copy of what they called their "Platform and Principles" is provided below. In truth, the leaflets were meant to intimidate the court and the peaceful citizens and, at the same time, to incite the ire of others. The leafleteers' motive was to scoff at the peace officers who were aware of the White Caps coming but retreated to their own homes, where they barricaded the windows with wool mattresses and pieces of furniture meant to keep the White Caps from barging in. The White Caps who rode into town that night wanted only to show the strength of their numbers in front of the peaceful citizens and to display their hostile and malicious intent.

Here is their first leaflet.

Our Platform

Whereas we do not want to be misunderstood by these present statements, we declare:

Our purpose will be to protect the rights of all people in general and the rights, in particular, of the poor.

We want the Las Vegas Land Grant to be adjudicated in favor of all those whom it concerns, and we maintain that it belongs to all the people who reside within its boundaries.

We don't want any more land thieves or obstructionists who might want to interfere. We are watching you.

We are not against attorneys in general, but the corrupt system they have used against the people must cease to operate.

The courts must understand that henceforth we will support them, but only when justice guides them.

The practice of using a double standard to deal with the people must cease.

The is a major difference between the laws of New Mexico and justice; and justice is the law of God, and it should be carried out at all costs.

We are opposed to racial distinctions, since we are all members, brothers, of the human race and all protected by the same glorious flag.

We favor all irrigation projects, but we will fight all efforts that try to monopolize the flow of water in a way that will injure the residents who live on lands that depend on these waters.

We favor all projects but reject any corrupt means used to advance them.

We do not care how much wealth a person amasses as long as it has been gained through just and honest means.

The people are now the victims of partisan politics, and it would be best if the politicians quietly guarded the peace. The people have been persecuted and mistreated in a thousand ways to satisfy the whims of politicians. They, as usual, continue in their ways. Retribution will be their reward.

We are closely watching these tyrannical despots.

We hold no ill will against any single person, but swindlers and tyrants are clearly our enemies.

We should have a free vote and fair counting of the vote, and the people's majority should be respected.

Intimidation and plans to bring suit are no longer effective tactics to use against us, and should the old way persist, we prefer death to suffering.

And for the right to live, we are willing to risk our lives.

If anyone doubts that we are law-abiding citizens, look how we suffer at the present time.

We will support anyone who does justice, but he who does wrong will face the consequences.

The White Caps

1,500 strong and growing daily.

4.

The poster with which we closed our last edition had the only effect of putting the sheriff and his deputies on alert and moved the sheriff to organize his forces and post armed guards inside and outside his home. He did this not to protect the lives and property of the citizens but for his own personal safety. Although the White Caps did not return to do their *drill* in Las Vegas, they did concentrate their efforts on destroying fences, haystacks, and railroad bridges for quite some time. They did these well-planned malicious deeds at night. With respect to the hundreds of miles of fence line they ruined and destroyed, we will only mention a few incidents to illustrate the point and not tire our readers, since these attacks are widely known. By now our readers have been able to read the platform as it appeared on the streets and as the platform of a new political party being organized by the Antichrist and his White Caps.

They endeavored to carry out the stipulations of that platform not through legal means but under the cover of their white hoods and by wielding axes, wire cutters, matches, and daggers, the indispensable tools of the White Caps in pursuit of their "lofty" goals and to uplift their platform, as they said, "no matter how high the cost."

10. "To New Mexico," Luis Tafoya

El Eco del Valle, vol. 6, no. 6, 10 February 1911,
Las Cruces, New Mexico

"A Nuevo México" ("To New Mexico") is a triumphal poem by Luis Tafoya (1851–1922) occasioned by the ratification of the New Mexico state constitution in 1911, a measure assuring that New Mexico would become the forty-eighth state of the union in January 1912. Like a number of his contemporaries, Tafoya was educated at St. Michael's College in Santa Fe and joined a cadre of emerging Nuevomexicano journalists that included Camilo Padilla, Felipe Maximiliano Chacón, and others who contributed to an emerging intellectual tradition by treaty citizens supported by local Spanish-language newspapers.

Several of Tafoya's submissions to local newspapers employ popular verse forms and mock dialogues of the kind that were part of a communal oral tradition that appealed to newspaper readers. In "To New Mexico," as befits the moment it seeks to enshrine, Tafoya employs the more formal metric associated with poetry thought to constitute high art, or *versos de arte mayor*. In this case, fourteen-syllable verses are laid out in *cuartetos* (quatrains) with consonantal rhyme, the resulting form referred to as a *sonatina*. Considered Tafoya's signature work, the poem foregrounds the widely held belief that New Mexico had reached a pinnacle in its quest for inclusion in the union, deemed the salvific means to curb de jure discrimination experienced by Spanish-speaking citizens and the means to reaffirm civil rights guaranteed by the Treaty of Guadalupe Hidalgo. In carefully crafted language and by drawing on his formal training in rhetoric, Tafoya produces an extended image that presents his fellow treaty citizens as an upright people imbued with noble bearing who have prevailed against adversity and discrimination.

Long after the momentous struggle for statehood and nearly forgotten, "To New Mexico" was declared the state poem in 1991 by the fortieth legislative session of New Mexico. For more on Tafoya's role in Nuevomexicano letters, see Meyer 187–88.

Work Cited

Meyer, Doris. *Speaking for Themselves: Neomexicano Cultural Identity and the Spanish-Language Press, 1880–1920*. U of New Mexico P, 1996.

To New Mexico

Lift your downcast forehead, New Mexico,
That clouds the beauty of your serene face,
And in elation take hold of that bright crown.
Symbol of glory, good fortune, and peace.

After so many years of struggle and insistence,
Your fate has changed, and you are victorious,

Finally arriving at that fortunate day
The high point of your good fortune and the fountain
    of your joy.

You once had been an empire filled with riches,
And you had to suffer through many adversities,
But now your triumph is whole and complete,
Your perseverance has secured your just reward.

Your people, alone and isolated, for three centuries
Defenseless, without help from any quarter,
Fought with daring and recklessness for their survival,
Paying in blood for dominion and rule.

And after such heroism you have finally merited
The fulfillment of the promise you so insisted could be
    yours,
So that you would be admitted to the union of the States,
And to the sovereignty that free men love.

Obstacles and setbacks vanish forever,
And you have your entry into that glorious union,
Where its citizens prosper and flourish
With many guarantees and great protection.

For this stunning achievement, your offspring say well
    done,
For this honor is so outstanding

And in this, your new sphere, we truly hope
That by the dint of your once imperial past, a great state
   you will become.

11. "New Mexico," Teles (pseudonym)

La Estrella de Nuevo México, vol. 2, no. 34,
26 March 1897, Socorro, New Mexico

"Nuevo México" ("New Mexico"), an editorial essay ap-
pearing in the Socorro, New Mexico, paper *La Estrella de
Nuevo México* (*The Star of New Mexico*), is signed with only
the pseudonym "Teles." The full context of its authorship
remains incomplete since only three issues of *La Estrella de
Nuevo México* are known to survive in library collections.
Was Teles an editor, or did he merely subscribe to *La Estrella
de Nuevo México*? Was he a columnist, or was he a casual ob-
server of the US border region? In the essay, the writer does
disclose that he immigrated to New Mexico, as he says,
from "nuestro México Viejo, el paraíso de nuestros ensue-
ños" ("our Old Mexico, the paradise of our dreams"), but it
is not possible to tell whether Teles was a frequent contribu-
tor to area newspapers, and little more has emerged to de-
termine the identity of the writer behind the pseudonym.

   The essay does proffer clues concerning the writer's
motivation for making his comparative observations (geo-
graphic, historical, sociological, and otherwise) between
New Mexico and Mexico. The two locations, Teles begins,
could not be more geographically dissimilar. He notes that
Mexico's lush semitropical climate, which he describes as
"[l]a floresta más privilegiada de América" ("the most fa-
vored garden of the Americas"), is dramatically different
from New Mexico's arid uplands and mountain valleys.
Teles notes that New Mexico is a land of deserts, frigid ex-

panses, and a severe topography where agriculture yields only the most basic means of subsistence.

Yet Teles also seeks to discover what elements explain the relationship of one land to the other and to register his appreciation for the place where he now resides, the generally lesser-known of the two lands. Since his essay is especially concerned with "la inmensa zona que pasó a dominio americano" ("the immense area that fell under American rule"), Teles seeks to know what elements tie one region to the other. He concludes that it is the people on both sides of the national divide that account for any similarities. Teles argues that a shared history harkening back to the Spanish colonial period has remained intact on both sides of the international border. New Mexico, he writes, "ha conservado con más fuerza las costumbres paternales de nuestros mayores" ("has retained with greatest intensity the paternal ways of our elders"). He further suggests that it has kept "[l]a relativa similitud del carácter civil y religioso de su pueblo" ("[t]he relative similarity in religious and civil character of its people").

An astute observer, Teles reveals the working of a trained mind, making it unlikely that the essay is the product of an off-chance submission to *La Estrella de Nuevo México*. Teles's observations, suffused with sociological and political descriptions, permit readers not only to see the contrasts between "México Viejo" ("Old Mexico") and New Mexico but also to appreciate the fact that a shared culture operates in both locations. In the end, this allows Teles to conclude that New Mexico "no es México, ni nuevo" ("is not Mexico, and it is not new").

New Mexico

Anyone who knows New Mexico, even if only by its geography, will not find any resemblance to the land of the Montezumas—that is, as is said here of "Old Mexico." Not in its sweet tropical dominions, not in its fertile fields, not in its splendorous skies, not in its always smiling sun, not in its calm moon, not in its soft stars: Mexico is Mexico. It is the most favored garden of the Americas, and, in this sense, New Mexico is a part of that world, but New Mexico is not Mexico, and it is not new.

And yet, if no topographic or geographic similarity can be had, one can indeed find many shared characteristics with Mexico in the matter of its Spanish colonial peoples.

Of all the immense area that fell under American rule, New Mexico is the region that has retained with greatest intensity the paternal ways of our elders, their simple and welcoming sympathy for others belonging to their race. A New Mexican will receive anyone calling at his door with open arms.

The relative similarity in religious and civil character of its people confesses to the familiar habits of another Mexico. The region, too, shared the name Mexico, although its deserts, its valleys, its mountains filled with snow, even its citizens, bereft of ancient palaces, were distinct. New Mexico is, after all, New Mexico, but it is also its brotherly people with the same outlook of those of our Old Mexico.

The mountainous geography of the territory is characterized by frigid zones and agricultural valleys. Its most populated towns—Albuquerque, Las Vegas, and Santa Fe—often drop below freezing.

And because the Rio Grande drops down from the arms of the snowcapped mountains and flows through a studded and very colorful region, as we travel across that region, we come upon areas like the Taos Valley dressed in greenery and paired together with happy townships.

In these mountains are other towns and mining camps, some of which have exclusively Spanish sections that are called "Spanish towns," where a peaceful and friendly way of life can be enjoyed and where we are sure their disgusting factories of misery have not yet been located.

There are also herds of cattle and wealthy ranchers who have large families and who are truly happy living in the old pastoral ways and who reach what seem like eternal lifespans and who go to the eternal rest of the grave with undue caring and resign themselves to the laws of nature. Those New Mexicans seem to live as they want and live as long as they want.

With us, no less, we have an example of this in Mister Juan Vigil, who now resides in a hospital in San Bernardino. An elderly man, he struts like a plump peacock through the streets at one hundred and ten years of age. He has not bowed his neck with the weight of so many years; he has not lost a tooth and does not suffer from digestive illness or weakness in his legs. This immensely privileged human being was feed and nurtured in the open and untrammeled regions of what is today the territory of New Mexico.

There are some places that are key to the future, especially a mining future, such as those in Sierra County, where all that is lacking are people to build all kinds of businesses. It possesses very rich, gold-bearing, quite exploitable placers and very gradual uplands that are loaded with wild rock moss that sheep and cattle can feed on, and there are accessible forested patches filled with timber. And it has springs of water that only need the hand of man to open them up and direct their flow across the surface of that virgin land.

Considering the severity of the climate, man and nature are only just beginning to see eye to eye, and things once thought impossible can now be overcome. In other terms, nature has become a friend of man, and it schools him in new ways. It tells him to apply his labor in those frigid areas, where there is no shortage of usable plants with which to make do until it is possible to see, if not a prodigious springtime, at least one that will yield harvest gardens filled with abundant root plants that can sustain life. Here plants such as potatoes, beets (and all plants of the species) will do well in areas where snowfalls are common, thus making the most of periods when there is no frost or ice.

A contingent of labor is sure to come to help move New Mexico toward the future it seeks. And the light of civilization has come over New Mexico's horizon, and its charming cities have been kissed by progress. Education and learning have powerful centers, like those in Las Vegas. Religion has its seat in Santa Fe, and every town is building altars to industry and knowledge.

And New Mexico, following its traditional habits, has not let the power of governing slip through her hands. The New Mexicans, those of the Mexican race, are still at the helm in honored positions and play a role in political matters. Because of this, their language prevails, and so, too, it appears that their sane customs and their social goodwill will continue to prevail. And the Spanish-language press maintains itself quite well, despite having only a handful of people in the community to count on, to protect and support it.

And it is because of these things that we are not ashamed to say from the heart that if tomorrow we were given the option to pick where we would want to live out our days to our heart's content outside our Old Mexico, the paradise of our dreams, we would not look to the Eden that is California, with its dreamlike forests and enchanting women: but, yes, we would make our home here. It is decidedly in this New Mexico, a place where our fellow countrymen still reside and where the pastoral ways of our ancestors continue to be found and where, despite the crudeness that has come to disfigure our language as it is spoken at present, no one rejects the use of the home language, a tongue that may be the best spoken that can be found under the sun.

12. "The Historians: The Need for a True and Exact History of New Mexico," Enrique H. Salazar

El Independiente, vol. 2, no. 3, 6 March 1895,
Las Vegas, New Mexico

Enrique H. Salazar (1858–1915) was a capable editor and a prolific writer who seldom failed to publish an editorial essay on the front page of his weekly *El Independiente* (*The Independent*). While still in his thirties, Salazar became a founding editor of *La Voz del Pueblo* (*The Voice of the People*), a newspaper first established in Santa Fe and later moved to Las Vegas, New Mexico. *La Voz* proved to have a phoenix-like ability to rise with renewed purpose at critical moments in its history. In 1894 Salazar sold his interest in *La Voz* and established *El Independiente*, which he published without interruption for the next thirty years.

Throughout his career in journalism, Salazar expressed deep concern over the increasing domination of public and social life that Anglo-Americans began to exercise in the region. Salazar continually reminded his readers that these newcomers had little regard for the history of the area but rather seemed bent on establishing their own cultural superiority and continuing with their economic and political appropriation of the territory.

Salazar energetically registered his concern over historical appropriation in an 1895 front-page editorial titled "Los historiadores" ("The Historians"). Salazar urges Nuevomexicanos to take stock of the importance of historical and social recognition. He appeals to historical precedent, insisting that Nuevomexicanos hold on to their participation in the new social order that enveloped them, reasoning that prior achievements authenticated Nuevomexicano claims to land, language, and cultural and civic rights. Salazar directly addresses the question of how the region's history should be told and why it is so critical that it be written from the vantage point of treaty citizens. Salazar argues that an accurate history would suffice to convince Anglo-Americans of the merit and worth of the Spanish-speaking population. Furthermore, he believes that Nuevomexicano achievement, tempered by noble and heroic acts, should ensure that present-day Nuevomexicanos not be subject to censure.

Salazar had taken nineteenth-century liberal ideals to heart. He believed that the historical record, if presented in full, would stand as an objective, impartial, and irrefutable witness, a final arbiter that would help treaty citizens recover from the ravages of conquest and dispossession. For Salazar, the merits of the Nuevomexicanos were evident and incontrovertible. An accurate account of their history, he believed, would be enough to convince Anglo-Americans of the right of Nuevomexicanos to full participation in social and political life.

With the publication of "The Historians" in particular, Salazar joined others of his generation in promoting a positive sense of community through literary and intellectual endeavor by examining the question of historical discourse in his journalistic work. For more on Salazar, see Meyer 102–08, 216–17; Meléndez 72–77, 110–12. For a full account of the internecine violence between Nuevomexicanos and native tribes referenced in Salazar's essay and in subsequent texts (entries 13, 14, and 31), see Brooks.

Works Cited

Brooks, James F. *Captives and Cousins: Slavery, Kinship and Community in the Southwest Borderlands.* U of North Carolina P, 2002.

Meléndez, A. Gabriel. *So All Is Not Lost: The Poetics of Print in Nuevomexicano Communities, 1834–1958.* U of New Mexico P, 1997.

Meyer, Doris. *Speaking for Themselves: Neomexicano Cultural Identity and the Spanish-Language Press, 1880–1920.* U of New Mexico P, 1996.

The Historians

A great many essays have been written since the year 1850 until today that propose to write the history of New Mexico from the time of the conquest until our times, and it can't be said that even one of these historian aficionados has possessed the qualifications or has had the knowledge and disposition required for such an arduous task. What's more, none of them have been up on the customs and inclinations of our people; none have even the most remote idea of the many important and transcendental events that have occurred in this land in various, different, epochs and that, if seen correctly, make up the true history of the people.

Those histories have limited themselves to reproducing, somewhat faithfully, some ancient facts about our history recounted by some writers who were contemporaries of those days and of the long interval of time that elapsed from then up until the conquest of 1846. They supply us with scant information that does not deserve to be called history or chronicle.

Equally defective are the accounts they give us from the year 1846 until now, since in sum, they limit themselves to raising up and referring to the deeds of the conquerors and do so without taking up the events, difficulties, customs, or the intimate lives of the true people of this territory, although they don't do so intentionally but because they are ignorant of all these points and have no inclination to study them. They have limited themselves to narrating a few facts known about some prominent people who entered this land at the time of and following the American annexation. Men who occupied some high post in civil or military service to the United States. This is quite expected, and we don't censure it since it was the only information accessible to these historians, who were not equipped to do deep studies and give brilliant accounts concerning the most salient and important points in the true history of New Mexico.

The most important of these histories and the one with the biggest literary pretension is the one written by W. H. Davis more than thirty years ago, and yet, its merits are scant. It contains so many errors and fictions and in so many places displays such partiality against the native settlers[46] of this land and their forebearers that its value as a history is entirely void, but despite this, it remains the source that has inspired all the subsequent historians who have attempted to write up the annals of New Mexico. It should be noted that even as they follow Davis, they do not match him in literary ability. From this we conclude that the history of New Mexico has not been written as of yet as it should be and that the field is wide open to someone who judges himself to possess the education and qualities needed to write this work and who can provide us clear and full information concerning events of the past and who can inform us on the transitions and vagaries that New Mexico has experienced in the three hundred years that have transpired since the first conquest and colonization by the Spanish. This task rightly belongs to a native son who, imbued with sufficient zeal and love of country, can take up such an undertaking and who, at the same time, is well-endowed with a work ethic, education, and training to be able to bring to light a history that is not filled with errors and lies and that places in evidence the facts concerning our ancestors, the obstacles they overcame, and the dangers they faced head-on and with perseverance over the course of three centuries. It should show how they lived in isolation and apart from for most of this time, without links or ties to the rest of the human race, and how they had to figure out how to govern themselves and care for themselves against the repeated aggressions and attacks from a number of Indian tribes.[47]

This type of history would provide interesting reading and would prove and place in evidence the consistency and daring of men of the Spanish race who, in a period of time when the railroads were unknown and nearly the entire continent was all but empty, kept themselves alive in a sterile and unhospitable land, surrounded by enemies and at a distance of more than two thousand miles from the closest civilized province with any foundation at all. These were the true explorers of this continent, and they cannot be compared to the Pikes, the Frémonts,[48] and other American explorers whose trips and explorations in the present century have been so pondered by the voice of fame but which are but child's play in comparison with the actions that the Spanish undertook more than two hundred years before.

So we hope that education and learning is now taking off among the children of New Mexico, that the day will come when we will not need to look beyond our own circle to find authors with enough education to write with due precision and clarity the history of our territory from the time of Spanish colonization until our days, so that the entire nation and our descendants can know of the deeds accomplished by their grandparents and of the events that came to be over the years and this, so all is not lost and relegated to darkness and so that people only recently identified with the territory are not allowed to monopolize the entire historical field that concerns the Hispanic-American race and entirely ignore those key events that preceded their arrival. It is right to present the facts as they are and not do an injustice to any historical figure who appears in the annals under the three separate governments under whose rule we have lived. Each period should be treated with the focus it deserves. This is what our history requires for it to be valued and accorded real worth.

13. "The Unvarnished Truth about New Mexico" (first section and continuations), editorial staff of *La Revista Católica*

La Revista Católica, vol. 3; nos. 30, 33, and 35; 28 July, 18 August, and 1 September 1877, Las Vegas, New Mexico

In 1850, two years after the ratification of the Treaty of Guadalupe Hidalgo, the administration of the Catholic Church in New Mexico passed from church authority in Durango, Mexico, to the Diocese of Baltimore, Maryland. The change established the Dioceses of Santa Fe and led to the appointment of Jean Baptiste Lamy, a French priest who would lead the new region as bishop. A few years later Lamy would recruit a group of Italian Jesuits to New Mexico and head up what came to be known as the New Mexico–Colorado Mission. Prior to leaving Italy, the Jesuits began to raise money for their mission under the misguided idea that they would be ministering to Native Americans, only to discover upon arrival that their work would be with the Spanish-speaking population, the largest population group in the territory. Once in New Mexico the Jesuits began to found parishes, schools, and colleges. Importantly, they also began to issue *La Revista Católica* (*The Catholic Review*), a weekly paper in Spanish that reached Mexican communities north and south of the international border. Inasmuch as these incoming Jesuits spoke Italian and possessed a distinct culture, they felt little compulsion to disturb the cultural practices of the Nuevomexicanos. Even though they took some issue with local religious culture, they were more tolerant of it than the incoming Protestant clergy, who began to filter into the territory at about the same time. The Jesuits immediately began to exert their influence in matters of public education. Not only did they learn Spanish, they also encouraged its use in the classroom and came to be staunch defenders of the interests of the Spanish-speaking community. As a result, Nuevomexicanos established a close-knit bond with the Jesuits based on shared spiritual, religious, and cultural affinities. Anglo-Americans, however, took great umbrage at what they considered Jesuit meddling in the education of New Mexicans. Anti-Jesuit sentiment ran high in English-language newspapers, which charged the priests with trying to incite the ignorant masses of New Mexicans to challenge the public education laws of the territory. Anglo-American legislators in New Mexico were adamant that curbing the influence of the Jesuits was imperative to securing their design for an American-style curriculum in the public schools. This set the stage for a bitter conflict that went on for decades, with the two opposing camps resembling their predecessors in the colossal religious struggle in Europe that followed the Protestant Reformation.

La Revista Católica worked to refute Anglo-Protestant critiques of parochial education and to refute the Spanish Black Legend,[49] particularly the history of encounters between missionaries and indigenous groups during the three centuries of Spanish colonization of the Americas.

The paper routinely concerned itself with social conditions in the territory, paying special attention to trends that threatened to alienate the region's Spanish-speaking majority from the core markers of their group identity: language, religion, social mores, and ritual observances. In the opinion of the editors, the greatest damage came from the denigration the Nuevomexicanos in the English-language press and from views held by certain experts from the East who characterized New Mexico and the Mexican community as indolent, ignorant, superstitious, and generally backward. In a five-part series of editorials (three included here) titled "La verdad sin rebozo sobre Nuevo México" ("The Unvarnished Truth about New Mexico"),[50] the Jesuit editors at *La Revista Católica* sought to shed light on several social, economic, and political problems that had emerged in the twenty-five years since the American takeover of the region. In these essays, the editors show solidarity with the New Mexicans by fending off accusations from the English-language press. At various points, the editors praise New Mexico's agrarian beginnings and the untrammeled way of life common to Mexican ranchers and sheepmen. They so insist on the benefits of pastoralism that they raise it to a kind of trope that stands for what they qualify as "una elevación de ideas y de sentimientos" ("a set of high ideals and positive outlooks"), which they hold up in contrast to the ravages wrought by waves of unscrupulous economic speculators, or "bulliciosos" ("noisemakers"), hailing from the industrial states of the union who "se aprovechen de la miseria de pobres familias" ("take advantage of the misery of poor families"). For more on *La Revista Católica*, see Meléndez.

Work Cited

Meléndez, A. Gabriel. "The Social Apologetics of *La Revista Católica*: Church, Race, Gender and Mexicanidad." *Women and Print Culture: A Critical Exploration of the Archives of the Border Region of Mexico and the United States*, edited by Donna M. Kabalen Vanek and María Teresa Mijares Cervantes, Arte Público Press, 2021, pp. 97–130.

The Unvarnished Truth about New Mexico

Not too long ago *The Pueblo Chieftain* and *The Santa Fe New Mexican* were pulling at each other by the hair. *The Chieftain* was tossing stink bombs at *The New Mexican* and calling us semi-brutes, saying that we know neither justice nor morals, that we are backward and behind in intellectual and material civilization, and so on, and so on. All this, it declares, is due to the men of the Santa Fe Ring who run, administer, and control everything in the territory. By contrast, *The New Mexican* appears to be the obvious defender of those Santa Fe gentlemen and intends to show us how lucky we are to be enjoying their beneficence, since they have ushered in peace, tranquility, and the noble justice that prevails in this country. They have also brought forth the civilizing effect of progress over the past twenty-five or thirty years, and so on, and so on. Gentlemen, let's not exaggerate!

We do not doubt that only good intentions motivate the editors of these two newspapers to spend so much time and effort discussing this territory. *The Chieftain*, no doubt, as it reminds us, is New Mexico's best friend, even if it appears to treat the poor New Mexicans harshly, but it surely only does so to comply with the guidance coming from sacred scripture: "Those I love, I reprimand and punish." We are convinced that *The New Mexican* works at nothing other than to defend the honor of the territory. It's clear that it believes what it preaches—no doubt here. The editors of the paper firmly believe that it is thanks to the rule of its Santa Fe bosses that we are advancing in every category of material progress and learning, that justice here is respected, that property and lives are secure, and so forth. But by exaggerating their claims, they weaken their own reasoning.

Here we are not as immoral as *The Chieftain* makes us out to be. If the New Mexicans are quiet and law-abiding, this is not the result of the good administration of the territory, as *The New Mexican* holds forth.

Now, let's note how these observations have been constructed out of a mix of very fragmented elements—for example, morals, superstition, material and educational backwardness, the character of the people, the administration of justice, and so forth—making it difficult to get anything out of such a skein of items. All this talk of the Santa Fe Ring really doesn't bother us. We have been hearing about the ring for some years now. The current territorial delegate spoke about the ring as part of his platform, and still we have yet to learn which ring members form part of his cabinet. In the row between *The Chieftain* and *The New Mexican*, some federal officials serving the territory are named. As far as we are concerned, we are content to use the dispute to speak the unvarnished truth regarding the current condition of New Mexico and that of the New Mexicans.

We do oppose the naming of individuals in this story. Our reasoning is that the question is much more general and should not be restricted to narrow parameters.

When *The Las Vegas Gazette* published some articles in which the temperament of the New Mexicans appeared in a favorable light, one Santa Fe reporter replied by feeding *The Chieftain* with one of the usual articles damning the Mexicans and scoffing at the editor of *The Gazette*. It seems that making fun of the editor was much easier for this reporter to do than to overturn the ideas held by our colleague in Las Vegas. The arrogance of *The New Mexican* in referencing these articles is just as laughable as going on to shred them to bits for singing the praises of the people of New Mexico and then to all the while claim that this is owed to the present administration of the territory.

Indeed, what do Governor Axtell and the Santa Fe Ring have to do with the virtues that bejewel the character of the New Mexicans? And if there be some blemishes amid sounder qualities, it would be unfair to credit them to those gentlemen. But let's leave this journalistic tomfoolery behind.

If some of the nations that call themselves civilized but in reality are riddled with the unending chaos of business

III. NEW MEXICO: NOT NEW, NOT MEXICO

and other matters would truly like to see a pastoral form of life, they should hurry and come visit New Mexico before the very structures that hold sway over them arrive here and change the place forever. And, please, don't come here as did one traveler, whom we wrote about in the *Revista* last year, who came only to spend a few days in Santa Fe or some other town with some friends and then abruptly returned to the United States. This tourist did nothing more than listen to a certain group of bearded men who portrayed themselves as wise and knowledgeable but who have poop for brains.

These same men think they have a right to opine willy-nilly on everything and to judge and to put down a people without having taken the trouble to examine things carefully. But let them come here to live with the Mexicans for a few years. They might prefer those parts of the territory that are thought to be the least civilized as they gather insight on what is a pastoral way of life. They shall see that this life is not one of barbarity or stupidity, and they will know that if there be civility among businessmen, they can see that civility redounds to ranchers and sheepmen, making evident that if the former activity, business, attracts noisemakers, the second, ranching, attracts those who are tranquil and quiet. For years and years, the simple and hardworking way of life on these immense plains has come from the noble blood that runs through the veins of the Mexicans, from their traditions and the religion they profess. These elements have tempered their character in such a way that those who know them intimately can't help but admire their way of life. While the New Mexican is docile and complies with the laws, he is not at all servile, and so great is the spirit of independence in him, some conclude that it borders on haughtiness. He lives and works with few needs, and greed is foreign to him. His generous nature is at times excessive, and, thus, he shows little regard for money. Poverty does not debase the most abject of the New Mexicans, who, though dressed in rags and living in a hut, manages to maintain a set of high ideals and positive outlooks, virtues that have inspired great admiration in us on more than one occasion: his patience in adversity, his hospitality, his love of family, his respect for his elders, and more are qualities that no one can take from him. Of course, even these many fine qualities are mixed in with defects, some of these quite serious. We are aware of them and have no need for others to constantly bring them up, as they are apt to do in conversation, in books, in articles, or in letters to the foreign papers. We should note here that none of these pamphleteers really know these defects or can size them up as we are able to do since few of them know this community as we priests who minister to it. These defects emerge from the very abundance of their good nature or from the way of life that can be had here: ignorance, immorality, a disregard for improving one's state in life, apathy, etc. These and other vices will not surprise anyone who knows this land and its history. They are in general the same vices that are found in other people whose primary livelihood is pastoral, though we acknowledge that in this land it has reached outlandish proportions. This does not surprise us, nor should it, given the lack of concern on the part of the government of Mexico (and we might add) of Washington for improving things here. We shall now take up these defects in turn and in the manner that they are hurled at us, and by this we hope to truly shed light on the real conditions in this territory.

How can one expect that an entire population be educated when it's a known fact that this country does not have, has never had, and will likely never have any important urban centers and that its people have been and will likely continue to be spread over an immense stretch of land? Those who assume that knowing how to read and write is sufficient instruction for a people imagine a network of schools at work, strategically located in the various precincts of each county, each imposing on parents the obligation to send their children to them. These people believe this system will take care of every problem. Not so, gentlemen. A people are educated generally, when it is found that they converse, in private or in public, with educated people. Knowing how to read and write (as regards the masses of people) is not the principal means to become educated. We insist, if this were so—knowing what this land is like—why does it surprise anyone to know that the people are ignorant? Those familiar with this land are surprised to learn that so many people here know how to read and write and that a large section of the population strives to receive an education. We should also add that we have received lovely reports from many Americans themselves, folks who have lived here for long periods and know the New Mexicans quite intimately and who speak of the wide circulation of *La Revista* among them. We affirm this free of any fear of being unmasked, for in regard to knowing how to read and write, etc., people here are not behind the farming and grazing communities in Europe. And, yet, we do not doubt but rather affirm that the most needed form of learning is absent here, and therefore we conclude that the peasants of Europe are better instructed than folks here, even if they don't know how to read and write, and even though we insist that these are the most-needed skills. What does it matter to a poor shepherd or a glum farmer that he knows how to read? Where would he find the books that he needs? And how would he manage to obtain them? Moreover, what good is it to read books if he cannot comprehend them? As is so often the case, no book can be understood before having acquired some knowledge of science and letters that most commonly is learned by word of mouth. What's more, those books with the greatest circulation in general do not deal with subjects that are of interest to a poor man, a worker, a farmer, a shepherd, and so they are not of much use to him. There are countless proofs that books are not the principal or only means to educate the popular classes, although they can be and often are an important help in cases when the people are instructed beforehand. It can be said that for the masses of people, learning and science (if provided in the degree that is useful) propagate in the same way that faith traditions do, *Fides ex audítu*, "faith comes from hearing," as Saint Paul said. Faith is propagated by hearing. It is by listening that the majority of people acquire their religion; by listening that they learn the first principles in morality, also by listening that they learn what are the laws of their nation. These things all make for a good citizen and keep him free from the entanglement of lawyers, and it follows that by hearing he learns of the best practices in agriculture and horti- culture—by hearing comes instruction for all things per- taining to one's profession, etc.

Inasmuch as it is the case that the truly learned will al- ways be a minority, we can conclude that the propagation

of useful forms of knowledge depends on urban concen-
trations of population. Have such concentrations existed
here up to now? No. Will they or can they come to exist?
Well, who can say for sure? So then, what is there to gripe
about, and why are we constantly put-upon by those
"wise folks" who come here from the United States? Why
do they never tire of throwing in our face the matter of
ignorance? To sum things up, since these have been, are,
and will be the conditions in this land, where the edu-
cation of the popular classes is very difficult—perhaps,
some might say, impossible—the strangest thing is to
dwell on how backward learning is among the New Mex-
icans and not on how it is that they have kept a desire to
become educated burning in the midst of such obstacles
and difficulties. (To be continued)

(Continuation)

Let's now take a look at another smudge that is heaped
on the character of the New Mexicans and which is said
to be the cause of an exorbitant corruption of the habits
and customs that (allegedly) reign in this land. Protestant
ministers stand out among those who make this claim
and who have come to this territory to evangelize, but
not having managed to achieve much, it appears they
want to spew the bile they gather by defaming the country
in their sermons and in their little books and in articles

that appear in the newspapers in the United States. So it must be. These gentlemen call themselves ministers of the Gospel, and it's not surprising that they arrogate to themselves the right to thunder against the vices of the people. We ask, do they do this out of jealousy? Who can know? If such jealousy exists, might it be unguarded spite? Perhaps, but we will be patient. Let's not get too hung up on this point, since it seems the case that exhortations never really change things but paper over things with a kind of hypocrisy, which does not help these hypocrites but rather advantages, without doubt, the communities in which they reside and where they want to cause scandal, at the very least, be it that these communities should think to rise up to repudiate them.

For us, the strangest thing to see is the high number of men with no other mission in life than to spit in the face of the New Mexicans and build up a bucket of filthy accusations so vile and so shameful that we hate to repeat them here. It suffices to say that in letters and articles sent to foreign newspapers or (as we have seen) in small books set before a readership that is hungry for scandal, nothing is off-limits—not class, not family, not sex. They besmirch the honor of women, of youth, and of men of every standing. If these gentlemen who come among us and insist that they are the regulators of public behavior and then take it upon themselves to accuse us publicly of immorality, it should not surprise anyone if we beg to ask, What is the public behavior of our accusers? If we were to honestly judge, as does every court in a civilized society, we would not admit without scrutiny the testimony of a man that is not respected, and most especially if the accuser is acting on his own.

In truth, the matter recalls what we hear in chapter 8 of the Gospel according to John, where the scribes and Pharisees who feigned great care for the morals of the people found fault in a woman who was taken to Jesus and, surrounding her, ask him, "Master, this woman has just been found to have committed adultery. Moses in his law has commanded us to stone such women. What do you say about this?" It is true that our divine Master sought to keep silent and avoid giving an answer, but as the scribes and Pharisees insisted on questioning him, Jesus told them, "He among you that is without sin should take up stones against her." This was a divinely inspired answer and one that would go on to be a maxim for all Christian people.

Gentlemen reformers and jealous guardians of good morals, it is far from us to excuse sins and excesses. However, if the lack of morals among the New Mexicans so offends you and *if your conduct is without fault, cast the first stone against them.* The newspapers in the States are full of your communiqués. We have seen your magazine articles and your pamphlets, all written with hate for the men and women of this land. We permit ourselves to ask, Who are you all that rise like righteous preachers on questions of morality?

Filthy immorality abounds here. This is so and can't be denied, but who is responsible for it before God and men? Let our readers be the judge. Just before and not long after the conquest of this land, troops of men, in a manner of speaking, invaded this territory. It is difficult to speak of them without feeling indignation. They were men without families or men who had left their families behind, God knows where. Men without means, but men seeking fortune by any means possible. Men without religion but intent on reforming the religion of the people residing here. These men quickly sought to be baptized, although they did not believe in the practice, and to assist priests that they despised and to build churches they did not attend. When all is said and done, they were men without morals or principles. Some deemed them "the pioneers of civilization in the far West." Oh, what a beautiful civilization they have brought us! Just imagine, dear readers, the damage these men have caused to a simple people of little learning but of an open and generous heart. The truth be known, persons like these are now absent from this land. A few stayed on, and we have known some of them. When we have asked, they have said they are amazed that any amount of morality, honesty, and shame have managed to continue to exist. They, too, more so than others, deplore immigration, which to their way of thinking has been excessive, if only for the fact that more immigration has brought with it improvements in everyday behavior, which has caused them to change their own degraded ways. Even with them gone, however, this did not end the work of demoralizing a people. And we dare to say that the military forts were not far behind any other institutions, since by following the bad example their commanders exhibited, the soldiers acted badly and with free reign, whether among the Indians or among the Mexicans. Then add to this the high number of single men who did not want to return to the States without first having made a fortune, but who, on the other hand, did not want to set roots here because of their dislike and lack of respect for New Mexico and the Mexicans. Nothing has contributed more to the decline in morale in the territory than the high number of rootless foreigners in this land. They always remain foreigners, and it follows that they looked on New Mexico as a land they came to only in pursuit of money. We have known more than a few of those bachelors who have filled the land with vice and sickness. Some have even feigned to marry, and later they have left their wives and families after heading off to places where it is near impossible to find them. Others of this same ilk have come and duped the daughters of good and honorable families, using the influence of such families for their own benefit, and Lord knows why these Americans have held such sway over the native people.

In another issue we will speak of the misery that afflicts the greater part of this community. We hope to be able to sufficiently explain the cause of it. For now, we can say that this misery is the work of disreputable dealers (mostly foreigners) who are the principal cause of the corrupt behavior that now rules here. Our readers should pardon us if we only briefly comment on this point. What type of unscrupulous men take advantage of the misery of poor families in order to destroy them? This kind of thing is seen in all nations, and we believe that this is why God will turn the fortune of even the most powerful families to dust and why he will often punish the sins of the fathers in the sons. But here, in this land, for the reasons we give above, this baseness has reached gigantic (unbelievable) proportions. Here poverty has had its traffickers, and they, in combination with Yankee northerners, have for years and years managed to extract wealth from the poor. Then, too, are the vices of those single men without families who arrived here and provided large and sure benefit to the mercantile stores. It appears we are speaking enigmatically at this point, and many of our readers may not understand us. But we must declare that our pen drops from exhaustion, and we can't insist upon this more.

This being the case, how can these hypocritical foreigners be so bold as to throw dirt in the face of the native people? Who, if not you, are the principal cause of so much vice and corruption in the territory? Truthfully, not a single American now residing in New Mexico should be bold enough to talk, much less preach on the immorality of the natives of this land.

Now permit us with all the respect we can muster to address those most sanctimonious ministers of the "pure gospel." How can you claim in sermons, assemblies, pamphlets, and newspaper articles that Catholicism is the main cause of the corruption of this community when the most shameless scoundrels here are non-Catholics? If you manage to see some modicum of modesty, humility, and honesty, if this land is still not like other Protestant countries in matters of morality, this is due to the Catholic faith that has resisted the devastating currents of such infamy and thanks to which we are able to proclaim alongside the prophet, "it is an act of God's mercy that we have not been devoured by all things" (Lamentations. Jeremiah 3.22).

In truth, although we have much to deplore, readers should not believe everything is exactly as said regarding the morals of this land and as has been written by denigrators in the newspapers. In one of these small books, among the most scandalous, we read, "moral corruption has impregnated everything to the core, even and without exception the best families, since not one of them admit entrance to certain foreigners." We believe the reasons for this are easy to ascertain. If the immorality of this region were to be compared with that of some cities and regions of the States—take, for example, Chicago— these same Americans residing here would claim that by comparison the territory is ahead by a hair in terms of morality. It is true that in the States a certain German American business owner with knowledge of both the States and this territory has observed that the deepest and most radical moral corruption is to be found among the Mexicans. This, no doubt, is why those used to a certain decorum abroad cannot entertain the idea that often the most corrupt behavior is papered over by hypocrisy.

In addition to the cause we have already mentioned, there are others we have not mentioned, only because we don't wish to drone on or because we believe them to be secondary concerns. There's the matter of a certain Protestant minister who pointed to the lack of education and religious instruction, if not of secular instruction, and who recommended an increase in the number of public schools. It's the case that the very same Americans who heard him mocked him, and with good reason. We would commend the abovementioned minister to Governor G. Brown, a non-Catholic, who, in an address to the seventh National Convention of Teachers in St. Louis in August 1871, said, "It is commonly said that education is the biggest defense of republics against vice and immorality. However, that theory is not borne out by deeds. The most refined of ancient and modern civilizations have been the most perverse, and in our own age, the biggest scoundrels have been the most highly polished scoundrels." He later says, "It's understood that here I am not speaking about moral or religious education but of education that is only of the intellect (profane instruction), of the kind that is conducted at present in the schools." (To be continued)

(Continuation)

With respect to all that has been said in favor of or against New Mexico, what has most often been addressed concerns the material progress of the land. If someone in the States were to continue to read what the newspapers here, or in Colorado, publish on this topic, no doubt he would end up more perplexed and confused than at the start of the reading given that the judgments and views of journalists are so diverse. These views hinge on the different ways of seeing the subject—better yet, on the different ways of understanding material progress. If the well-being of the New Mexican had only to do with good roads, easy means of transportation, stores fully stocked with luxury goods, swift communications with the States, etc., it could be said that the territory is much improved and will continue to improve over the next few years. It's very likely that within months we will see two railroads reach the territory—one from the North, the other from the South. They will unite us with the eastern states and with Texas and California. Yet we feel we must note that these things are not sufficient measures of the prosperity of the land, since Mexicans who have lived here for years and even many Americans repeatedly tell us, in terms of material well-being, things were better at the start of the conquest than they are at present. There was more industry here, a greater abundance of money, trade flourished. As the Mexicans like to say, "There was more gusto to living."

What's the cause of such drastic change? Could it be the very annexation by the United States? But how is it that, whereas annexation brought so many advantages in California and Texas, it only brought misery to New Mexico? And how are we to understand that this land prospered more when it was subject to a nation where the norm was civil discord than now, when New Mexico belongs to a nation that enjoys peace and appears to be so advanced? Add to this that in times past, this land— settled some three centuries ago—was attacked by many tribes that would not broker for peace. They impeded any form of commerce. Now, in our own time, the territory looks nothing like it did then. And yet, despite the long history of civilization and barring the near destruction of the Indians and despite having become a part of a nation flourishing with industry and commerce—one that enjoys complete peace—the New Mexico of some forty years ago might have been seen as relatively prosperous and rich but now is one of the poorest countries in the Americas. Our readers should not think that we exaggerate the matter. Nothing urges us to do so other than our experience and our interactions with the poor who we encounter through our pastoral duties, as is our obligation. We find cause for concern in the unwavering testimony of both Mexicans and Americans in the territory and the debates that surface from time to time in the newspapers concerning the subject. If a reporter or journalist writes something to contrary, it could be that he wants to hide the truth and more easily win over readers with his ideas, or it might be due to an ignorance of what really goes on among the poorest families in the land. These gentlemen are foreigners who have a peculiar way of managing to speak about things they know nothing about. What's more, everyone is aware that in this our "blessed" territory, Americans and Mexicans are two separate people. They are totally different and divorced, one from the other, and maintain no communication or inter-action between them. So, it is not hard to find men who are completely unaware of the conditions of this land, even if they have resided in New Mexico for many years.

The causes of the great misery, as we have discovered and others have informed us, varies. Here we will mention only a few of the most observable. First is the lack of industry in this community. We do not intend to speak of commercial industry tied to large manufacturing that requires large capital investment and a network of investors. No, we speak only about home industries, activities that should be in every home and in the fields. These are livelihoods that may not make one wealthy but that always lift up the well-being of every family, regardless of how scarce their means are. So, alright, this kind of activity is unknown here. The old Mexicans who knew and practiced them lament their absence and loss. Men between the age of forty and fifty have an unclear understanding of them. They recall as children seeing their countrymen engaged in domestic arts that now are lost, and they remember their parents busy at work in tasks that are unknown today. Even the names of such things are forgotten. As concerns the young, they have no idea of this industry, and should they read these lines, they might think to themselves, "Home industries! What is the *Revista* getting at with this notion?"

Before moving on, we want to reply to the whining of the usual weeping hypocrites. We have become accustomed to their remarks: "These surely must be Mexican Catholics! They know nothing of work or industry!" To people of this ilk, if we could find some free of prejudice, we might ask if by chance they know of a more industrious people than the French or the Belgians or the French Canadians. And indeed, they are Catholic. However, we need not leave the region to fend off such accusations. Among these same New Mexicans, where the domestic arts are absent, well before those same critics arrived to blind us with their false idea of civilization, they were a very industrious people. If not, how did they manage to maintain themselves for a period of three hundred years, surrounded by enemies, stuck, as we might say, in a "desert" without a means to communicate with civilized nations, other than Mexico, a country with which they could only hope to preserve the most difficult and infrequent relations? To describe the state of domestic industry in times past in New Mexico, we need to go into detail of the kind that might seem irrelevant but that are quite important and that we believe will not turn off our readers. So, a brief and general description of the topography of this land is needed, if only to serve those readers in the States and in Europe who honor us by reading the *Revista*.

A traveler from the East—from, say, Kansas City—comes to this territory after having crossed the rich and fertile fields of eastern Kansas and enters a desert, and not a desert of fine sand, as the name could suggest, but rather an area of grass-covered plains rich enough to maintain herds of cattle. And still, it is a desert because it lacks water and because it receives little or very infrequent and unreliable rain. These grasslands rise to some seven or eight thousand feet above sea level. Nearing the Rocky Mountains, the number of water sources (rivulets, creeks, rivers) increases. Next to these sources of water, some populated pockets can be found, and people there supply themselves with wood from the forests and with water from the rivers to irrigate their fields. It would be otherwise useless to hope to raise crops without any kind of artificial water source in this area. The middle of the region we are describing is New Mexico. In earlier times, before the good communication we now have between New Mexico and the States existed and when California and other northern regions were held by Indians, New Mexico was boxed in and had almost no communication with modern nations. It was therefore obligated to support its people with what could be harvested from the land. This was not just for a year, but for centuries, something that makes this land one of the most ancient associated with the American union. Back then, New Mexico had inhabitants only along the bank and near the confluences of rivers on the Rio Grande. Above all, it was a country of herdsmen, since much of its energy was given to raising livestock. It's a fact that the New Mexicans had to defend their flocks from the incursions by Indians, and it's also true that these incursions are what most contributed to the slow progress of this land. And yet the constant skirmishes did not prevent the gradual increase of the size of the flocks, which would become the real source of wealth for this country. The New Mexicans tried in other ways to extract what they needed from the land. Cotton was raised here. Its fiber was woven and made into rugs and serapes—American blankets cannot match them in quality. Candles and soaps were manufactured along with a thousand other useful items, making it unnecessary to import them, as is now the case. There were a goodly number of cobblers, blacksmiths, carpenters, tailors, and hatmakers, all trades now in short supply given the considerable increase in the population at present. Gold fields and mines operated, and the hunting of buffalo and antelope was bountiful, and the grasslands were not denuded of these useful animals, which came about through the greed of inept hunters. This kind of hunting, at that time, was a major source of wealth. In addition to providing a very delectable meat source, it supplied hides for export, an activity that is now unknown.

From these descriptions our readers can see that in times past, some industry existed here, and the land provided nearly everything needed to live. Of course, these activities were in their infancy, and they could have and should have been perfected. We are not speaking of luxury goods; as we have noted in an earlier article, this was largely a pastoral society. There were, however, families that were not content with corn gruel and wool fabrics, nor with mules as a means of conveyance, etc. These families ordered chocolate, silk, carriages, and other higher-cost items from Mexico. However, at the time, exports from the country outweighed the value of items imported, and the relative prosperity of this place came in other ways. We will, however, speak of this matter in a future article. (To be continued)

IV. CITIZENS BEYOND REPROACH

14. "Twenty-Four Reasons Why the Natives of New Mexico, or the Mexicans, As They Are Called, Should Vote for the Constitution and Form a State," José Desiderio Sena

El Nuevo Mexicano, vol. 1, no. 9,
27 September 1890, Santa Fe, New Mexico[51]

The prominent Santa Fe resident José Desiderio Sena (1867–92) sent an editorial to his hometown newspaper in Santa Fe as he neared the end of his life. Known to his neighbors as Major Sena, having served on the side of the Union in the American Civil War at the battles of Valverde and Glorieta, Sena helped defeat and drive out the Confederate troops bent on taking over New Mexico. Sena had the rare opportunity to study law in Alexandria, Virginia, after which he returned to New Mexico, making use of his proficiency in English and Spanish in his law practice. He went on to hold several public positions in territorial government, including a position as registrar of the land office.

Sena's "Veinte y cuatro razones" ("Twenty-Four Reasons") appeared in print some forty-two years after the signing of the Treaty of Guadalupe Hidalgo and gives voice to the grievances shared by treaty citizens that the implementation of the treaty's guarantees had waned after decades of territorial rule and that the full measure of their civil rights had not been realized in daily practice. Harkening back to the treaty, Sena urges his fellow New Mexicans to continue to struggle for the protections of their language, religion, culture, and claims to property and to attain the fullest expression of those rights by backing efforts to make New Mexico a state of the union. For more on Sena, see Meléndez. For a history of the statehood movement in New Mexico, see Holtby 14–23.

Works Cited

Holtby, David V. *Forty-Seventh Star: New Mexico's Struggle for Statehood.* U of Oklahoma P, 2012.

Meléndez, A. Gabriel. *So All Is Not Lost: The Poetics of Print in Nuevomexicano Communities, 1834–1958.* U of New Mexico P, 1997.

Twenty-Four Reasons

1. Because it's now time to demand of the government full compliance with the promises it made to incorporate us into the brotherhood of the American federal union of states and to admit us as true citizens of the United States, as stipulated in the Treaty of Guadalupe Hidalgo, the greatest inducement that we could have been offered so as to embrace the rights of citizens of the United States and to renounce those we had as citizens of the republic of Mexico.

2. Because a people who in full knowledge and with complete desire renounced its rights given by a government free and equal to that of the United States, in the hope and promise of bettering its condition, is

entitled to a measure of respect and to the strict ful-
fillment of the promises that have been made to it.

3. Because it is well-known that at the time the govern-
ment of the United States took us in and placed us
under a territorial form of government, it did this in
full knowledge and trust that although we possessed
Mexican nationality we possessed all the needed
qualifications in terms of loyalty to the nation, valor,
obedience, ability, honor, and integrity so as to be-
come citizens of the United States.

4. Because a people of a distinct nationality and living
under the infamy of a territorial government who
notwithstanding goes out onto the battlefield to meet
the invader who threatens the nation with destruction
and, in doing so, expels the invader from its bound-
aries in complete defeat such that he would not dare
return and then continues to demonstrate loyalty to
the government, love for American institutions, and
obedience to the laws and the authorities as properly
constituted should be and by rights must be entitled to
the sovereignty that is owed it as a free state.

5. Because a people who have passed their own laws
under a system of territorial governance and drafted
by talented Mexicans born, raised, and cultivated in
their own land and whose laws have been ratified

without exception by the Congress of the United States is highly capable and perfectly competent to live under a sovereign state government.

6. Because the people of New Mexico have and hold in their very bosom the talent, capacity, honor, integrity, intelligence, valor, patriotism, and all that is necessary for self-government and, moreover, to govern a pack of imposters who come among them and dissent so as to deny the Mexicans their rights and besmirch them by denigrating and subjecting them to the vile charge of being incapable of self-government.

7. Because the sons of Hidalgo, Morelos, and Iturbide,[52] just like the sons of Washington, have never been slaves but plainly free and independent subjects.

8. Because the Mexicans love equality and sovereignty and acknowledge these things as the only means to demand their rights when trampled upon and the true fulfillment of the promises that the government has made to them.

9. Because a people who through nearly four hundred years has fought, maintained, and defended its rights and honor, and has defended with equal valor and patriotism its families, its property, and country against the unjust incursions and raids by nomadic Indians and has withstood these fierce traumas, is capable and able to govern itself.

10. Because the Mexican people are of noble heart and generous and liberal and what they desire for themselves, they desire for their equals.

11. Because the people of New Mexico recognize that the privilege that comes from self-government is the biggest prerogative given by God and affirmed by our republican form of government.

12. Because the people of New Mexico possess abundant mineral, pastoral, and agricultural resources that, if properly developed, will allow them to accumulate immense wealth.

13. Because the Mexicans are anxious for the government to turn over tutelage of the lands that belong to them so that they can establish educational, agricultural, charitable, and correctional institutions.

14. Because the Mexicans want the government to turn over, as it promised, goods and property that have been stolen from them by the Indians.

15. Because the Mexicans want the government to pay them for their military service rendered during the Civil War and the goods commandeered by the army during the same period.[53]

16. Because the Mexicans want a law passed that will compensate them for all the injuries to their property during the invasion and occupation by rebel troops in the years 1861 and 1862.

17. Because the Mexicans want the quick adjudication of land grants legitimately granted to their ancestors by the governments of Spain and Mexico and to avoid the many ravages to their lands that come from the neglect of the government, which has retarded the adjudication of these grants by treating them separately and outside of the public domain.

18. Because the Mexicans do not want their territory and residents therein sectioned off to create new territories or to enlarge the size of existing states.

19. Because the Mexicans condemn in the most strenuous terms every dark defamation that devilish imposters have used to try to discredit this people and this land.

20. Because the Mexicans maintain that their love and respect for the honor and virtue of the nation was transferred to them by their ancestors and knows no rival.

21. Because the Mexicans love liberty, peace, and public tranquility and obey the law and promote progress.

22. Because the Mexicans love and sympathize with all men, irrespective of their origin, the color of their skin, or their nationality, in accord with the worth of their character.

23. Because the Mexicans abhor all imposters who arrive with a smile on their face and try to use them as instruments for their own aggrandizement.

24. Finally, because the Mexicans honor and will always stand ready to respect the rights of every individual in accord with the respect they are shown.

In conclusion, in these brief statements of reason, I express what has always been my view, and so I must say that the Mexican who casts a vote against the constitution, for political gain, hate, or personal vengeance or for personal gain or in the hope of personal gain, is a false son of New Mexico, a traitor to his homeland, and the assassin of the most sacred interests of the people of New Mexico.

I respectfully submit my reasons to the clear and honest consideration of every native that wishes to see New Mexico as a star in the constellation of stars that adorn the banner of stars and stripes, that glorious symbol of freedom.

Long live the natives of New Mexico, those noble sons of Hidalgo, the glorious father of independence, and the adopted children of Washington, who with ballot in hand will march up to the ballot boxes on election day, 7 October 1890,[54] and by voting for the constitution will once and for all establish themselves as worthy of the sovereignty they desire and capable of self-government and amply responsible to uphold state government.

15. "The Warrior Spirit: The Military Fire That Persists in Certain Parts of the New Mexican Populace," Enrique H. Salazar

El Independiente, vol. 4, no. 51,
3 March 1898, Las Vegas, New Mexico

16. "Ballad of the New Mexican Soldiers," Hilario Valencia

El Nuevo Mexicano, vol. 30, no. 28,
23 January 1919, Santa Fe, New Mexico

"El espíritu guerrero" ("The Warrior Spirit") is another editorial column by Enrique H. Salazar that addresses the condition and status of New Mexico's treaty citizens. As evidenced by José Desiderio Sena's "Veinte y cuatro razones" ("Twenty-Four Reasons"; entry 14), Nuevomexicanos were never comfortable with the idea of an ascribed citizenship that made them citizens in name only while subjecting them to discrimination and unequal treatment in the land they considered their homeland. As treaty citizens, they worked to assert their rights and to assert their standing in public life. Still, throughout the territorial and early statehood periods, the arrangement provided enough agency to allow Nuevomexicanos to maintain home rule at the level of precincts and counties and in the territorial legislature. Not altogether satisfactory, the arrangement gave treaty citizens enough ease to feel a sense of security in those communities where they were the demographic majority. Still, ascribed citizenship could not always shield them from the economic, political, and institutional machinations of elite power brokers in the Anglo-American community. Despite the guarantees stipulated in the Treaty of Guadalupe Hidalgo, in practice, Nuevomexicano loyalty to the Union and their ethnic status were often weaponized as a means of questioning their fitness as American citizens. In cases of conflict between individuals or within communities, derision and retribution gave way to violent and destructive reprisal. A period of calm returned when each group reminded the other of how the power-sharing arrangement was supposed to work for the benefit of all.

At specific historical moments, Nuevomexicanos found themselves having to defend themselves collectively from xenophobic charges of being a foreign, unassimilable people who remained out of step with the values of the nation. Three such challenges ensued: in 1898, with the outbreak of the Spanish-American War; in 1916, with the possibility of US military intervention in Mexico; and in 1918, with the advent of World War I.

The sinking of the USS *Maine* in Havana Harbor in 1898 reverberated across the nation. In New Mexico it occasioned charges against the Nuevomexicanos that they might hold hidden loyalties to Spain given the three hundred years of rule and deep cultural ties forged during the Spanish colonial period. Salazar's "The Warrior Spirit" addresses the first conundrum and takes issue with the charge of disloyalty, going to great pains to point out that whatever ties Nuevomexicanos had to Spain, they were sufficiently removed from those ties as to render them inconsequential. Salazar displays terse pragmatism that allows him to make absolute distinctions between the political realities of the present and the inheritances of a former time. Perhaps too sanguine for many, Salazar opines that charges of disloyalty should be a nonissue, insisting in his essay, for example, that there was not a single individual living in New Mexico who had been born under Spanish or Mexican rule. Nuevomexicanos, he deduces, could realistically look only to the United States as the country to which they bore allegiance.

A second geopolitical dilemma surfaced in the months ahead of a raid on the border town of Columbus, New Mexico, led by the Mexican revolutionary Doroteo Arango (Pancho Villa) in March 1916. This time the matter of disloyalty hinged on perceptions in some quarters that Nuevomexicanos had never completely severed their ties to Mexico. The English-language press seized on the opportunity to indict the Spanish-speaking community as treacherous and unreliable. Such accusations circulated widely and emerged with enough insistence that members of the Nuevomexicano community felt compelled to respond.

As the war in Europe continued into a second year, Nuevomexicano youth under the threat of conscription were encouraged to join the military. In conjunction with efforts at the national level, a sustained campaign to increase agricultural production in rural parts of the United States induced New Mexico farmers and ranchers to do their part to aid the nation and help secure a victory over Germany.

Service to country, patriotism, and public duty were widely esteemed in the greater Mexican American community of the Southwest. In New Mexico, notions of duty and sacrifice were often voiced by popular verse makers who spoke from personal experience as participants in the war effort. Such is the case with "Corrido a los soldados de Nuevo México" ("Ballad of the New Mexican Soldiers"), submitted to *El Nuevo Mexicano* in January 1919 by Hilario Valencia, a resident of Pecos, New Mexico, twenty-five miles southeast of Santa Fe.

The ballad narrates encounters between young men in rural villages and recruiters sent from Santa Fe to pull them into the ranks of the army. The verse maker relays his ideas in a *corrido*, or ballad, a form in the *arte menor* tradition consisting of *cuartetos* (quatrains) of eight-syllable verses in consonantal rhyme. Valencia's verses were meant to be sung and may well have been intoned by the recruits as a way to entertain themselves and take stock of their new circumstances. The experience of being torn out of the secure enclave that village life provided is registered from the unique perspective of those in the ranks of the recruits. The balladeer is one among his fellow neighbors who is able to name each person, thereby individualizing them and lending power to this intimate portrait voiced in song. This is a perspective that sharply contrasts, for example, with the lofty, patriotic tone and triumphalism found in Felipe Maximiliano Chacón's poem on Nuevomexicanos serving in World War I (entry 18). For more on the career of Salazar, see Meléndez 72–77, 110–12.

Work Cited

Meléndez, A. Gabriel. *So All Is Not Lost: The Poetics of Print in Nuevomexicano Communities, 1834–1958.* U of New Mexico P, 1997.

The Warrior Spirit

The destruction of the warship *Maine* and nearly all its crew has given way and will probably result in an armed conflict between the United States and Spain. A majority, made up of the most active, warmongering element of the great American nation, are crying out for a declaration of war with Spain, believing or feigning to believe that the maritime disaster that destroyed the American ship was caused by a Spaniard or a Spanish sympathizer, someone who took this action to satisfy his hatred of the United States. Such a supposition, though extreme and unproven, has fueled a pretext, an excuse, that those elements noted above desired to cause a breakdown, since over the last three years, they have been pestering the government to intervene in Cuba, even if it leads to war with Spain. At present, the natural antipathy of the Americans against the Spanish has spun off its axle and has become a universally uttered detestation echoed by the press, voiced in the pulpits of certain denominations, and heard as the public outcry of mobs in large cities. If the actions of the United States were to depend on this faction, there would be no waiting on a declaration of war. But the United States is one of the most learned and civilized countries on the globe, and this learning and civilization, along with its tradition of peace and abstention coming from Washington and the founders of the republic, impose certain duties that cannot be tossed aside. The government, led by a president as wise and honorable as William McKinley, who embodies the honesty and the energy of a George Washington and the wisdom and political sharpness of an Abraham Lincoln, must satisfy the whole of public opinion and establish the justness of a cause that requires extreme measures. This obligation does not derive from subservience or fear of other powers but from a sense of self-respect and the integrity of a government founded on high moral purpose. Because of this, neither the government nor any reasonable and caring group among the people of the United States can uphold an act of aggression against a friendly nation without an abundance of evidence for doing so and only under these conditions.

Now concerning the probability of war or peace in the present crisis, we say that it all depends on the investigation that is underway regarding the disaster of the battleship *Maine*. If the committee of navy officials finds that it was caused by an explosion that went up in the hull of the ship, then all uncertainty is removed, and there is no likelihood or possibility of war breaking out with Spain, but if the investigating committee declares that the explosion was caused by external means and that a bomb hit the side of the ship and caused the destruction, then the situation is extremely dire. This does not mean that there will be a declaration of war on the part of the American government right now but that Spain will be made responsible for the trouble believed to have been caused by one of its citizens, and at once an indemnification of six or seven million dollars in reparations will be demanded for damages caused. Spain, violent and prideful as it has always been, and still is, will care little about the amount claimed but will make much about the stain that marks it as responsible for a felonious act and a nation capable of an unheard-of treachery never before known on the peninsula or in Cuba or in any other Spanish colony. The Spanish government will see that it must declare war immediately or face a popular revolt with dire consequences for the government and for the Spanish monarchy.

In this eventuality, war will become a reality. The Spanish constitute a terrifying adversary because of their valor and physical preparedness and their formidable navy. They could also count on the help of some of the great European powers that harbor hate and rivalry with the United States. For these reasons our government will have to quickly prepare for a conflict to stay ahead of all the resulting complications and to deal with the fact that the first war cries would cost no less than fifteen million dollars. This is a small amount for a nation with the immense resources that America has at its disposal, but it serves to demonstrate the degree and shape that these preparations might take. One of the first and most needed actions will be the promulgation of a proclamation from President McKinley calling for the recruitment by the government of a million or five hundred thousand volunteers to be drawn up out of the various states and territories of the American union. We think it most likely that it would be for five hundred thousand volunteers, in which case the territory of New Mexico would need approximately ten thousand men, so that our region is well-represented on the battlefield.

It's lamentable that our fellow Hispanic American citizens will be obliged to take up arms against their brothers, the Spanish, but the matter is unavoidable. No other path is open since by birthright they are citizens of this great American nation, and as such it is their duty to always step up in her defense and under every circumstance. Fate or happenstance has caused New Mexico to be a part of the United States, and her citizens have become identified entirely and for the future with the destiny of the American nation. For this reason, neither blood relations nor sympathy stemming from a common history with the Spanish conquerors and colonizers of New Mexico or with their own ancestors can for one instance cause us to doubt our obligations and loyalty to the government and country we belong to and which has provided us with the liberty and privileges inherent to the American nation.

It's not strange, then—in fact, it's natural—to see that the warrior fire that burns in New Mexican youth is being rekindled by the rumors of war that circulate everywhere. There exists genuine fervor to take part in the defense of the interests of its homeland. Such expressions are extremely honorable and show that valor and loyalty are not foreign sentiments but values owed to the nation that has protected it and covers it with its flag. We think that the youth of this era, intelligent and educated, will serve with great honor and bring credit on the battlefield, equal in valor and daring to that of the valiant Anglo-Saxon. Intelligence and a responsibility to duty are what inform the valor of our soldiers. If cowardice and disaster have in prior times muddied the military fame of the New Mexicans, such things are not an inherent deficiency or the real measure of our gallantry. Ignorance and stupidity disfigure what ought to be man's most sacred duty. A spirit of emulation shall boost the spirit of the New Mexican volunteers and will make them equal in daring to their Anglo-Saxon comrades, and both shall fight with equal valor, should they, while en route to Cuba, encounter a fleet of Spanish warships on the high seas attacking their transports, or should they find themselves storming armed Spanish bunkers in fortified cities or entering the impenetrable forests of the Cuban island. They will heroically face exhaustion on that deadly island with its many deadly illnesses such as yellow fever, beriberi, smallpox, and others that are a death sentence.

War with the Spanish will bring hunger, death, and bloodshed. Even though our ground troops and our navy will initially suffer some setbacks, victory by the United States in such a war is certain and inevitable since this country has more wealth and men than any other to prosecute this war. The valor of the sons of a disgraced Spain will be ineffective and useless against the push of an unstoppable American force. Those few New Mexicans that survive the dogfights will come back to their nation covered in the glory and honor, a testament to their valor and patriotism in the defense of their home-land.

Ballad of the New Mexican Soldiers

Nineteen hundred and seventeen,
That's, gentlemen, when this starts,
Folks going about recruiting.
And picking only the flower of youth.

Liberto left out of Pecos,
Vigil is his family name,
Then, too, Genovevo and Juan Valencia
And, I must not forget, Miguel Roybal.

Now we go on to Colonias,
I can just recall those living there.
One was Isidro Quintana,
There was Paulino and Alfredo, all three.

Tomás Bowles also went,
He was another of those volunteers,
For Cándido and Tomás Armijo,
The Virgin of the Rosary, be invoked.

All of them volunteered.
And they signed on with valor

To serve their government
And its flag of tricolors.

There comes Juan Gómez
He's coming up in his car,
Recruiting volunteers
and sending them off to Santa Fe.

He goes on to tell them, "Let's see,
Gentlemen, who all will sign up today,
To serve the government
In the National Guard?"

All the wretched mothers,
Are drenched in tears,
Just thinking of the fate
That awaits their sons.

"Step this way, my son,
And kneel down at my feet,
So I can give you my blessing
Along with that of St. Joseph."

The volunteer soldiers,
Have gone off to drill,
And walking by their side
Goes a heavenly angel.

They take them to Santa Fe,
Since this is the capital
They take them to the barracks,
And there they'll start to train this very day.

Now they each take up their rifles
And they are put to help with tasks
So that they might begin their training
And learn how to shoot.

On the fourteenth of June,
The day they are to leave Santa Fe,
All the people weep,
As they follow them to the depot.

First, they took them to Albuquerque,
And put them up on some high ground
And placed them in camps
And kept them marching and drilling.

On the sixteenth of October
They left for California,
Even the rocks seem
To note their absence as they departed.

The train whistle blew at departure
Help us, Eternal Father,

They're going off to San Diego
To serve the government.

It's the volunteer soldiers,
That now are wearing a crown
And I trust in the Holy Child
That they return with victory.

Farewell, family and friends,
An entire generation
Is going to defend the land
And to hold on to their honor.

Mother, Virgin of Guadalupe,
I have come to finish this ballad,
I am Hilario Valencia
that's how I sign my name.

17. "Mora County Has the Largest Group of Volunteer Agricultural Workers," Antonio Lucero

El Nuevo Mexicano, vol. 28, no. 42,
3 May 1917, Santa Fe, New Mexico

In 1911 the Nuevomexicano historian Benjamín Read described Antonio Lucero (1863–1921) as "one of the most brilliant citizens of New Mexico" (488). Read's assessment drew on more than mere talk. He rightly could point to Lucero's many accomplishments as a journalist, teacher, and public servant. For over three decades Lucero had worked as an associate editor of *La Voz del Pueblo* (*The Voice of the People*) in Las Vegas, where he contributed many editorial essays and columns to the paper. Lucero served several terms in the New Mexico territorial legislature and was elected secretary of state once New Mexico had gained statehood. His dossier expanded when he assumed a position as professor of Spanish at New Mexico Normal University (today New Mexico Highlands University). There he taught large cohorts of Spanish-speaking New Mexicans, sharing with them his love and knowledge of Spanish and Latin American literature. He also served as a member of the Normal University Board of Regents.

Lucero's interest in and contributions to the education of Nuevomexicanos gained him access to regional learned societies such as the Archaeological Society of New Mexico. His membership in Anglo-dominated civic and social organizations was a rarity at the time and provided him with a unique opportunity to claim ground in the battle for cultural recognition that treaty citizens had been engaged in for decades. The Archaeological Society of New Mexico issued *Old Santa Fe: A Magazine of History, Archaeology, Genealogy and Biography*, a serious and rigorous publication founded and edited by Ralph Emerson Twitchell, the leading historian of the Southwest at the time. The magazine catered to an Anglo readership, but when Lucero was made associate editor, readers were introduced to his considerable skills as a writer and editor. Lucero was often asked to do talks for the edification of members and guests at luncheon meetings of the Archaeological Society. On these occasions, Lucero would regale his audiences with memories of his boyhood spent in a remote ranching village halfway between Las Vegas and Santa Fe, New Mexico. In bringing forth these experiences, Lucero sought to educate Anglo-Americans on the cultural values of his community. Lucero recounted how daily acts of survival fostered a powerful sense of community. His talks harkened back to a time and place where virtuous acts of kindness and sharing among relatives and neighbors compensated for lives filled with adversity, privation, and hardship.

Lucero maintained that the greatest disfigurement of his people's experience had come about because of ignorance, in the best of cases, and denigration, in the worst. As the preparations for war took hold in New Mexico, Lucero took every opportunity to highlight how Nuevomexicanos in rural New Mexico expressed solidarity with the nation by enlisting in the military and by contributing to the war effort on the home front. Lucero seems to take special pride in his ability to speak well about his fellow treaty citizens and does as much in his report on Mora County, published by Santa Fe's *El Nuevo Mexicano* at the outset of World War I. In this piece, Lucero reiterates how the heroic farmers who lived in the county were taking every opportunity to increase their agricultural yields as part of their commitment to demonstrating their loyalty and patriotism. For more on Lucero's public career, see Meléndez 86–87, 201–03. For the biographical sketch that gave rise to praise of Lucero, see Read.

Works Cited

Meléndez, A. Gabriel. *So All Is Not Lost: The Poetics of Print in Nuevomexicano Communities, 1834–1958.* U of New Mexico P, 1997.

Read, Benjamín. *Illustrated History of New Mexico.* Translated by Eleuterio Baca, New Mexico Publishing, 1911.

Mora County

They are plowing and transplanting every acre, going up the flanks of the hills and even the front yards of their homes, according to an announcement by the secretary of state, Antonio Lucero.

Mora County[55] has what is arguably the biggest volunteer labor force in the state, and the news brought to Santa Fe by the secretary of state, Mister Antonio Lucero, is that the people there are plowing and planting every available acre of arable land, even those on the flanks of the hillsides and those in front of their homes. Mr. Lucero gave a speech about efforts for war preparation to the people of Mora last Friday night and upon his return to Santa Fe made the following report on his trip to Governor Lindsey:[56]

As you have requested, I take this time to inform you that on Friday the twenty-seventh of this month, I traveled to the town of Mora by car and gave a speech at the courthouse that evening before a crowd that filled the court chamber and left only standing room for others in attendance.

My topic was the war effort in all realms of industrial activity as the means to successfully face the crisis that confronts our nation at the present time because of the part we have been forced to take in the world war. This is the same crisis that demands the attention of all the civilized world.

Judge Leahy[57] and Misters Larrazolo,[58] Ward,[59] and Voorhees[60] also addressed the audience. As I suspected, a large proportion of the farmers from the Mora area already had at least a vague notion of the circumstances of a world that faces a world war, and everyone attending the meeting appeared very grateful to hear the speakers as they brought forth the circumstances that have forced our nation to take part in this horrific conflict.

Mora County, one of the oldest areas of the state, is a county whose people are and always have been part of the working class, people who as a group have always contributed to the aggrandizement of New Mexico. Because of this, when I first set out to Mora, I fully expected to see a great deal of activity among the farmers, yet, even as I fully expected this, I confess with all sincerity that what I saw in the valleys I traveled through on the road to the county seat exceeded all my expectations.

For miles and miles and on each side of the highway, the land was cultivated and planted, to the point that there is not a single inch of arable land that is not planted, including the flanks of the hills and the front of many homes. From what I saw and what I learned from the citizens of Mora, it has what is perhaps the largest volunteer labor force of farmers in the state, and, in my opinion, neither the federal government nor state government needs to worry about Mora County. I am convinced that barring an extremely bad year, this county will be in the lead in the fall and will break all past records for production in the history of the county.

I did not visit the eastern side of the county, but I did speak to men from that part of the state and learned from them that the cultivation of those lands is proceeding much in the same way as what I saw happening in the valleys. As you know, the eastern end of Mora County is made up almost entirely of uncultivated land, like the rest of eastern New Mexico. I have been told that many more acres of land can be put into cultivation if farmers can obtain some form of financial help, be it from the state or from individuals. These farmers have told me that they possess the land and the energy to work it, but they have no seed, nor the money to purchase it. Still, beans and corn can be planted in those lands.

18. "Ode to the Heroes," Felipe Maximiliano Chacón

Obras de Felipe Maximiliano Chacón: Poesía y prosa, imprint of *La Bandera Americana*, Albuquerque, New Mexico, 1924

19. "To Miss Adelina Otero-Warren," Felipe Maximiliano Chacón

Obras de Felipe Maximiliano Chacón: Poesía y prosa, imprint of *La Bandera Americana*, Albuquerque, New Mexico, 1924

To say that Felipe Maximiliano Chacón (1873–1949) came from a family who cared deeply about the Nuevomexicano cultural legacy would be an understatement. Chacón's father, Urbano, published a newspaper in Santa Fe called *El Anunciador* (*The Crier*) in the 1880s. His uncle, Rafael, who was born in the period before US annexation, had been present when the American general Stephen Watts Kearny marched into Santa Fe in August 1846. Rafael would serve in the New Mexican militias established during the territorial period. He fought the Confederate troops at Valverde and Glorieta. When he reached old age, Rafael dictated his memoir to his son Eusebio, who diligently edited his father's recollections and distributed them to family members as four typed manuscript copies. Eusebio Chacón (entry 2), Felipe's first cousin, was a well-known writer and held public office in Trinidad, Colorado. Felipe's daughter, Herminia, taught in the rural schools of New Mexico and later assisted her father with the work of publishing his newspapers. Felipe's name had figured in Spanish-language newspapers since as early as 1894. Felipe himself had been at the helm of several papers over his career, but it was only after he assumed the job of general manager and editor of the newspaper *La Bandera Americana* (*The American Flag*) in Albuquerque that he began to write poems that he would later publish in 1924 in *Obras de Felipe Maximiliano Chacón: Poesía y prosa* (*The Works of Felipe Maximiliano Chacón: Poetry and Prose*).

Included here are two of his poems that speak with particular force to the condition of treaty citizens. In "Oda a los héroes" ("Ode to the Heroes"), Chacón pays tribute to the first generation of conscripted Nuevomexicano soldiers, young men whose first language was Spanish and who had never stepped outside New Mexico. These young men were pulled out of villages and towns and sent to fight in Europe in World War I. As with other texts in this section, the principal goal of the work is to celebrate the valor and commitment of this community in the face of the most dire and difficult moments in its history. It also aims to inscribe the story of the community's sacrifice into the history of New Mexico.

In both poems Chacón follows conventions of the *arte mayor* tradition. In "Ode to the Heroes," he employs eleven-syllable verses and eight-line stanzas, a poetic form known as the *octava real*. In "A la señora Adelina Otero-Warren" ("To Miss Adelina Otero-Warren"), he retains the eleven-syllable versification and makes a slight modification of the stanzas, breaking them up into *cuartetos* (quatrains).

The second poem is dedicated to Adelina "Nina" Otero-Warren, a native of New Mexico, the first woman candidate elected to Congress, and a leader of the women's suffrage movement in New Mexico. The poem defends the idea that Otero-Warren's qualifications and aptitude for holding national office are equal to those of men and argues that she would make a superb representative.

Maximiano shares his cousin Eusebio's penchant for stylistic conventions drawn from Latin American modernist and neoromantic trends in poetry (entry 2). Like Eusebio, he indulges in lexical complexity, but across his corpus of poems he is able to modulate his choices in accordance with the subjects (lofty or ordinary) he chooses. "Ode to the Heroes" is filled with archetypal images derived from classical Greek and Roman mythology, which allow the author to raise the stature of his personal heroes, boys he saw grow up to be the conscripted recruits sent off to World War I. Likewise, in the poem he dedicates to the suffragist Otero-Warren, he crowns her with august laurels in anticipation of her impending political triumph. For more on Chacón and Otero-Warren, see Nogar and Meléndez 39–41.

Work Cited

Nogar, Anna M., and A. Gabriel Meléndez, editors and translators. *El feliz ingenio neomexicano: Felipe M. Chacón and Poesía y prosa*. U of New Mexico P, 2021.

Ode to the Heroes

—*To the American Legion*

I.

With my spirit brimming with pride,
Amid the joy of victory,
I praise your valor in song.

You have my undying admiration,
For I am witness to your eternal glory
Your deeds, left yonder on the fields of struggle,
Are now a part of history.
Your loyalty, evident and consistent,
Burns bright over the Sunshine State.[61]

Our world twisted in anguish
At the action of a shameless tyrant
Who razed the tempestuous earth;
In vain that Prussian sought to satiate his fury
Ravaging the churches and homes of Belgium and
    France
And then, Germany horrified the world
With the cruel butchery that was the *Lusitania*.[62]

The cosmos is filled with horror,
Seeing how the blood of innocents turns Neptune's
    waters red

And behind them, the Teuton's hard fists
Drum out these evil deeds.

Assassin, destroyer of homes,
Violator of beloved mothers, daughters, and wives,
Given to wild abandon that makes a mockery of what
   is pure.

Growing and rising from the depths of the sea,
Wrenching cries drown the soul;
Civilization itself saw its foundations shake,
And heard the cries of a thousand *Brenos*[63]
As they lament,
"Oh, pity now the conquered!"
They threatened as they roared in fury
As they sought to erase, crazed with mad temerity,
The very soul of democracy!

Thus passed days and weeks,
And the months turned into years
And the despicable Teutons increased
Their inhuman submarine battles;
And bit by bit their insane forays
Violated America's rights
Such that Usona[64] issued its immortal proclamation:
"Shoulder your arms, for thy homeland calls thee!"

II.

Then and there is when you answered
With American honor and resolve,
Then and there you stepped forward
To fight for the sovereign rights of men,
Offering to die to salvage them;
As you left behind your wife and children,
And your beloved parents,
Leaving them,
With your eyes turned toward your happy home,
    hoping that
It would hold, in loving care, your beloved,
You said "goodbye" and with the resolute brow
Of the Spartan your raised up the flag,
The stars and stripes of the nation you love.
"Here I am," you replied, your farewell tinged with
    honor.

And so, you go now marching, glorious warrior,
To the blare of the bugle that arouses the spirit,
You alight and take up the torch of justice following this
    noble cause.

The whole world receives you with hurrahs,
There will be no hesitation, no quarter given, no break
Now that you have left behind industrious crafts

To take up the cause of the liberty of nations;
You now give all praises to Mars
As you turn your cannons against the enemy.

And so you go marching now, glorious warrior
Going far to cross untamed seas to reach
France, where that country awaits
With hope and joy amidst the many reasons to despair.

Dense clouds darken the sky again,
And as the hordes of enemies grow
And advance in power through the forests,
Now shouting a mantra, "On to Paris!"
A depleted nation, France, is weakened and bogged
    down,
Hearing but not trembling at the chant
That taps out retreat to the warriors.

But the scene changes unexpectedly
And the morning sun, like some divine torch,
Peeks out, pouring out rays of hope
Seeming like a victory call in splendid, far-off summer
It's the first day of June and advancing from afar
Whose voices are heard rising up in military cadence?
What are these mystical stirrings?
The German hordes quake
As the sharp, resounding notes hasten upward

For a moment, the beating fury stops
And from indigenous and remote lands
An unknown and brave army is singing
With the rumpus of their trucks.

"Not until we have finished them off,
We will not retreat until we are victorious."

Flashes of light rise ever higher
Up from that fiery scene
Where you witnessed your exalted and strategic march
Blessed, as it were, on Mount Belleau,[65]
And where you heard the cannons roar with patriotic zeal.
There, sons of America, you were crowned with glory
And there, too, in the land of Pluto, god of the under-
    world,
Now the place of a horrific battle
The steel of your sword strikes like a raging hurricane
In triumphal struggle, and there the shadow of the great
    Washington,
Unmoved and daunting, appears among his noble
    offspring,
Striking fear in the German fighter, who retreats with
    his impious horde
Your bravery so great that the even the Hun in his way
Paid you honor, naming you "devil dogs" in his language.

With heads raised, proud, you go forth, sons of New
    Mexico,
Fighting in Château-Thierry and in San Miguel
Joined as brothers you advance, winning laurels of
    victory.

And the flashes of that burning world come back
Upon seeing the brazenness of your guns
And upon hearing the solemn vow
Not to quit until the enemy is finished off
And the resolve not to sound a ceasefire until victory is
    at hand.

Each blow of your arms
Crushed the emerging Germans
Forcing the enemy to sound alarm after each sure defeat
And the throne of the empire swayed
And hate heaped upon the world.
But then, the eleventh day of November arrived
And in one abject defeat the haughty Prussian nation
    tumbles
See how its crown rolls in the mud
And so, too, the kaiser,[66] like Nero[67] and Diocletian,[68]
Is mocked and disrespected by Bellona;[69]
The kaiser shamefully flees
And with him the flattened tones of a de profundis[70]

Are dragged through the worm-filled muck
Sighing as he goes, the glory of the world is fleeting:
   "Sic transit gloria mundis."

The conquest is achieved,
Your holy mission is complete
Consider how your victory is crowned
And becomes a glorious epic!

Oh, how beautiful the colors wave
From the flag filled with stars,
As the world, rescued now,
Sings universal, ecstatic praises;
And in you, the sons of this earth,
And you, New Mexicans,
Sons of this land,
With the valor of true Americans
Were victorious in formidable combat;
That Olympus which showers you
With a chorus of mounting hurrahs
Rains down upon you
A flood of glory.

To Miss Adelina Otero-Warren

—*Republican Candidate for Congress, 1922*

Your brow is encircled by laurels
And your name radiates honor;
Your star rises today over the threshold
Of a new day's triumphant dawn.

The world advances and so, too, human thought
And new things into this life are born;
Today reflects the morning light
Of a new dawn into which women are born.

Born into suffrage, as man's equal,
But a more spiritually elevated soul:
Her name tills in moral purity
And the earth profits through her labors.

This meritorious evolution,
Marking the elevated path of progress,
Will cover New Mexico in glory
By sending a woman to Congress.

Accomplished, capable, honorable
Of graceful soul and sincere heart.
She is here, proclaimed by her people,
The ideal lady, Adelina Otero!

Descendent of noble Spanish lineage,
And further, wholly American,
Yet, of what importance is this external garb,
For she who deserves such echelons!

Human greatness is not bounded
It is not limited by nation;
From on high its power emanates
And descends upon those whose beauty pleases it.

Yet this flattery is not meant for
The servile benefit of the ego.
Rather my lofty aim
Is to tinge justice with idealism.

Hear, hear! A toast! A pledge of joy,
And of gratitude from a progressive citizen,
Who sends you in this humble verse,
The salute of a sovereign people!

V. Schools for the Masses

20. "Speech: Made by Miss Remedios Analla at the Examination and Exhibition Held at Galisteo, New Mexico, under the Direction of Professor J. M. H. Alarid," Remedios Analla

La Voz del Pueblo, vol. 15, no. 24, 25 July 1903,
Las Vegas, New Mexico

21. "News from El Rito," María Rafaelita Trujillo

La Voz del Pueblo, vol. 3, no. 9, 5 April 1890,
Las Vegas, New Mexico

22. "A Private School," Porfirio Gonzales

La Voz del Pueblo, vol. 9, no. 31, 28 August 1897,
Las Vegas, New Mexico

As the territorial period progressed, it became clear to treaty citizens that the establishment of public and parochial schools in the territory was a welcomed development, especially considering the near universal absence of formal schooling that had marked their experience during the three centuries that Hispanics had been in the region. In the past only small, select groups of individuals, particularly the children of elite families, had been exposed to formal learning through instruction by private tutors, who themselves were a rarity and only to be found in larger towns like Santa Fe.

The arrival of both Catholic teaching orders (Jesuits, Christian Brothers, Sisters of Loretto) and Protestant mission schools created more opportunities for increasing numbers of young people to be educated in the primary grades. Knowing how precarious their social situation was and facing the reality that access to education involved personal and collective sacrifice, treaty citizens took up the challenge with great zeal.

The first two testimonials on the benefits of education in this section come from young female students who had been exposed to early learning in a loose network of rural schools that began to operate in New Mexico late in the territory period. A common practice, especially in parochial schools, beginning in the 1880s was to hold yearly end-of-the-year exams along with student recitations and award ceremonies that featured the accomplishments of the graduating class. News of these quite elaborate ceremonies was enthusiastically reported in the Spanish-language press, attesting to the importance treaty citizens attached to educational attainment.

The testimonials by Remedios Analla and María Rafaelita Trujillo offer evidence that the desire for learning was not limited to upper-crust families living in large towns and that schools were not intended to train only young men. Such testimonials frequently appeared in local newspapers and offer insight into the ways that education was reaching the most remote and isolated rural villages of the territory, where the light of schooling flickered precariously and often only intermittently. What comes across in these testimonials is how young people from the most abandoned sectors of the community appreciated and embraced their time in the classroom and how rewarding the experience was for these village children. Analla's communiqué offers as an example a young lady who had benefited from being a student of the rural *maestro*, or teacher, Jesús María Hilario Alarid (see entries 5 and 23). Analla declares that she owed her school achievements to her parents and, importantly, to Alarid, who taught her the art of writing verses. As a fitting tribute to her teacher, Analla closes her communiqué with some verses of her own inspiration, in which she notes the benefits of learning in both Spanish and English.

Porfirio Gonzales's "Escuela privada" ("A Private School") is at once a testimonial on what education has helped Gonzales accomplish and a sophisticated treatise urging youth to aspire to higher educational attainment. It appears Gonzales himself had been a student at the Jesuit college that operated in Las Vegas from 1877 to 1885. Gonzales joined the Jesuits and was a member of the order, serving for some two decades in Montreal. By the time he issued his proposal for a private preparatory school, he had left the priesthood and had returned to New Mexico. The curriculum Gonzales proffers for his school follows the methodology and course of study central to Jesuit education known as *la ratio studiorum*, a program built on the study of classical literature and philosophy, rhetoric, writing, recitation, and public oratory. In essence, the program invoked a strict humanities curriculum in combination with the study of mathematics and the arts and even extended learning to applied skills, such as bookkeeping, shorthand, accounting, and typing. Gonzales declares that his program of study will be slightly more advanced than that of the public schools and organized as a series of seminar-style classes. His vision of the school setting is bold, modern, and quite novel given the frontier-like conditions that prevailed in New Mexico at the time. Gonzales makes an exuberant pitch to Nuevomexicano parents and potential students, one deeply informed by his firsthand knowledge of issues affecting the Spanish-speaking community. Gonzales's training and the fact that he could teach in both English and Spanish brought him to the attention of educators and school administrators who sought him out for a position in the newly opened New Mexico Normal University in Las Vegas, where he helped organize the first training institute for teachers in 1898. In addition to his gift for teaching, Gonzales frequently contributed poetry, short fiction, and the texts of his speeches to *La Voz del Pueblo* (*The Voice of the People*) in Las Vegas. For more on Gonzales, see Arellano and Vigil 93–96.

Work Cited

Arellano, Anselmo F., and Julían José Vigil. *Las Vegas Grandes on the Gallinas.* Telaraña Press, 1985.

Speech: Made by Miss Remedios Analla

Ladies and Gentlemen:

According to the Holy Scripture, as is our belief and truth, as revealed by eternal wisdom and illuminated by the light of the Holy Spirit. Holy Scripture says, "In the beginning, when all was chaos, the spirit of God spread over the waters and the darkness. He, the Almighty, formed the light and separated it from the darkness and called the light, day, and the darkness, night."

When a child is born and springs out of the dark maternal womb into the hidden nature of the natural world, it acquires a small bit of understanding and remains in darkness, but step-by-step it will come to be illuminated by knowledge and reason.

What then is it that the child needs to understand things and distinguish between good and evil? Education, ladies and gentlemen. Education is the thing that brings up a human being to the level of men, who by their studies have become immortalized for their discoveries in the arts and sciences.

We, not long ago, were ignorant of the fruits of education, but now its light shines and brightens our future happiness, and now the current generation of young people will come to know high civilization.

In closing, I say:

Today I stand before you
For the first time,
And reading, not in our language,
But rather in the English language,
Keep in mind the few in this school
Who are able to translate
And now I want to say
That we will all soon learn how to do so,
And be able to translate
As we continue to study.
Leaving us with little more to say,
Except that I, Remedios,[71] and schoolmaster Alarid
Are here,
And what do you all think?
Is this work something you all like doing?

News from El Rito

By way of a personal letter that we received from El Rito in Rio Arriba County, we have information that the public school under the direction of the learned teacher there, Mr. Pedro A. García, has closed for the term and after having carried the students there to a glowing public exam. At the close of the program, the child María Rafaelita Trujillo, twelve years old and the possessor of very likable talents, got up from her seat and improvised the following words directed at her teacher, which we reproduce here because of their directness and the kindness with which the young girl expresses her religious upbringing, her obedience, and her love of education.

With the permission of my beloved teacher and fellow classmates:

The omnipotent judge of the universe, by his just design and wise determinations, has in this moment determined that I, in obedience to my beloved parents, verify news of my sad departure, as I distance myself from the sober and wise advice of my generous teacher and at the same time of the sweet company of my beloved classmates. This separation is due to the obedience I have to my beloved parents, to whom I will give my feeble efforts to help them in the domestic chores at my beloved home. I offer my most expressive thanks to my teacher for all the sleepless nights and trouble he endured to provide me with a needed education. I stretch out my hand to my classmates in a sign of my happiness, as I in the same breath say: Farewell, farewell, farewell.

A Private School

Toward the middle of September, Headmaster Porfirio Gonzales will open a private school in Old Town. It will be exclusive to a small number of adolescent boys, and the program of study will be slightly more advanced than that of the public schools.

Its mission is to initiate a course of study that picks up where the highest grade under the best instruction leaves off. In other words, the desire and intention of Headmaster Porfirio is to establish, as best as can be done, a school that will provide those young men who are slightly advanced in their studies instruction at the high school level; or business school and, by this, as happens at the private Normal schools.[72]

If he manages to interest the parents with children and, moreover, the young boys with the idea in mind that many young men will be entering school this year, as students they will break ground as they open a new and very ample arena for their future. In young people, all that's needed is consistency and enthusiasm to be able to get started on solid work. Enthusiasm births attention and the interest needed in any type of business. Indifference, the biggest enemy of success, pales before attention and interest.

Now, as concerns the parents, it's well-known that the best inheritance that a son can receive is a small amount of solid education. There is no head of household who, if able, would not sacrifice, if required, to educate his children.

This should be more the case here in New Mexico than in any other part, given the circumstances that we find ourselves in. We lag behind in the most important fields of education. Our lot is to have been incorporated to an educated nation, and we will for many years need to compete with them [Anglo-Americans] here in our own land and in all kinds of civil and commercial business dealings. Time will tell if we achieve success in this competition.

If we work at building our capabilities, if we strive to make ourselves equal, if we emulate them in the matter of education, we will do well, since a foreigner cannot outdo a Mexican in talents. (It will always be the case that merit shines in the end, although it may be only after secondary motives or motives that corrode or even motives that degrade us have lost their influence.) If we are lackadaisical in matters of education, those who are now young and not able to compete with others their age will also not be able to compete with them when they reach old age.

When speaking of the skills that a young Mexican needs to become a useful member of our society, we should remember that he should be educated not solely as an intelligent American but also as an intelligent and useful New Mexican citizen. Our community will continue to be politically under the government of the United States, and it is good that this is so, but he will not cease to be a Mexican, and as in our internal dealings in the territory, our language will never cease to be the common language, even as English will come to be as needed and useful as our own language. We will continue to find ourselves in the condition in which the Canadians have found themselves and still find themselves. They are a part of two conjoined nations, and necessity has obligated them to occupy the same territory, but despite being amalgamated politically, each of the two peoples, those who speak English and those who speak French, retain their own languages so fiercely that both become equally necessary, for commerce at the very least.

In addition, education should make us capable not only of dealing with the foreigner but also of dealing among ourselves, and in this endeavor our language will always be a necessity. If not, what will happen to us will be akin to what happens to some young people in the colleges in the States.

There they spend five, seven, or eight years in those American colleges and learn the English language quite well, and this is good, but owing to their youth, they have neglected their own language to such a degree that by this time in their lives they would have to seek out someone who could write a letter for them to send to their girlfriends in Mexico, since they would not be able to write a letter without it being shameful.

As a consequence, the young Mexican who will one day be able to stand up in the legislature of the territory or the state, when New Mexico becomes a state, fully capable of representing our people in the language of the government and following up by going before the people and speaking to them in their home language, whether in speech or writing and with knowledge and complete confidence, this is the one who needs to step up now and be in a small way what he wishes to be in the future. He must possess both languages perfectly and to the highest degree possible.

In business, because of our trading relationship with Mexico, the Spanish language is so necessary that the Americans take private lessons in many of the colleges of the East, as many among us who have attended those colleges can attest—for example, those who have gone to Saint Louis.[73]

In speaking of our schools, the annual reports must get to Washington sooner or later as part of the government's gathering of statistics. What reflects badly in these reports on our people is the neglect of our families in sending their children to the schools for the full length of the term and also the inconsistency of attendance by those children. Census data from all the districts, which must also go there [DC], provides the actual numbers of those attending and the number of days in attendance. For example, the census for a given district may list three hundred school-age children for the year. The teacher's report and lists at the end of the school year list one hundred and fifty children who still attend the school. There were eight months of school, let's say, and of the number of boys on the list, half only attended school for three months of the school year. Of these, another half of the thirty-seven boys remaining, half of them, or fifteen boys, come to school every day of the week, and the rest are reported as attending two, three, or four days a week. This most certainly is a sad situation for any group, and if this continues to be the case, the masses of our people will continue to occupy an inferior position. From such numbers our government leaders come to conclude and spout out what they hear repeated, here and there: that we are still not prepared to govern ourselves, that we are too "illiterate," that we still occupy a minority status.

This gives us cause to think. Our people in adulthood will be equal to what they are in youth. Every Mexican who takes to heart the well-being of his race must convince himself that he cannot deprive his son of a single day of schooling without causing an injustice. A personal injustice to an active boy.

Alright now, considering the kind of schools that can be found, the private school offers the most advantages. There one can find not only the emulation and competition offered by the public school but also the personal and individual attention that each student will have in this type of school. The educational system in a private school is also much more beneficial than in a public school, given that the method of study and recitation takes on the features of a seminar that involves all the students. Such a conference, when well directed, provides the advantages that were part of the oldest systems of learning that were found among the Greeks and Romans.

Headmaster Porfirio has absolute confidence that with the cooperation of the parents, he will be able to provide several boys with the level of instruction that they would receive in any college outside of Las Vegas.

The curriculum of the school, if he can carry out his plans, will consist of two grades. In one, the lower grade, grammar in both languages (English and Spanish) will be the foundation of this level. To this will be added original writing in the two languages, translation, etc.

At the other level, rhetoric and oratory will be the mainstays. At this grade level will come all manner of original composition in prose and poetry, reading and analysis of writers of both languages, and literature by these writers. In terms of mathematics, arithmetic will be given in the second half of the upper grade, and algebra in the first half.

Other secondary fields will consist of bookkeeping, shorthand, composition, elocution (public speaking in theory and practice), music, vocals and instrumentals, and French. These two fields are optional and cost extra if desired.

Again, I urge the parents to take to heart my suggestion. Headmaster Porfirio urges that, with the month of September nearing, their patriotic sensibilities awaken and that they fan the same desires that beat in the hearts of the Spanish, our ancestors. New Mexico will continue to remain in a state of tutelage even within the purview of our government until the reports from our schools stop providing bad annual accounts.

Each issuance of these reports can say so much in favor or against us. And this is the reason that in Washington they say we are ignorant and that we cannot hope to be citizens, and so we are left and so we will remain for many years without a voice or a vote, to be seen only as a discredited and useless people.

On the other hand, the young Mexicans from old Las Vegas rush to the schools in New Town but rarely manage to compete with the American boys, and the inability to compete leaves a boy defenseless and pushes him to a state of passivity and inaction and causes him to learn only, like it or not, what he gathers as hearsay but nothing more.

For more information about the school's location and hours, etc., parents can visit with Headmaster Porfirio prior to the third week in September.

23. "The Spanish Language," Jesús María Hilario Alarid

El Independiente, vol. 12, no. 24, 17 August 1905,
Las Vegas, New Mexico

Sensing the enormity of the impact that attempts to re-
move Spanish as a public language would have on the
people of New Mexico, Jesús María Hilario Alarid sought
to issue a warning to as many of his fellow Nuevomexi-
canos as possible. He thus emits his message in the poetic
form most recognizable and accessible to the populace, as
a series of *cuartetos* (quatrains), or stanzas of octosyllabic
verses in consonantal rhyme arranged in four-line stro-
phes. The *cuarteto* has the same structure and versification
as the *corrido*, or popular ballad, as practiced in the *arte
menor* tradition. Alarid's poem is a passionate defense of
the Spanish language and an invective against those public
officials who seek to proscribe its use in schools and in the
public sphere.

Alarid's poetic tone often varied across a repertoire of
works, modulated by either the somber and sober or jocu-
lar motifs he sought to display. Alarid's playful tempera-
ment in "¡Ay! Viene el ferrocarril" ("Yikes! The Train Is
Coming"; entry 5) contrasts with the serious message he
delivers in "El idioma español" ("The Spanish Language"),
a poem that appeared in print twenty years later.

Alarid addresses the more consequential topic of lan-
guage loss with a sufficient rigor that suggests that the

locomotives Alarid believed were about to trample his people were not only those of spokes and steam engines but also those of other equally dangerous hulks barreling down on Nuevomexicanos in the form of social, cultural, historical, and linguistic erasure.

The Spanish Language

Oh, lovely Spanish language,
What? They want to banish you?
I believe there is no reason
For you not to exist.

Castilian has its origin in Castile,
Setting a foundation
For the grammar of the Mexican
Who speaks it to this day.

Oh, but they clamor for it
To become a dead tongue,
Not that they come out and say so,
But it's sure they want to do away with you.

When the Mexican understands,
The maternal tongue
It will be easy for him to learn,
The language of the government.

And why, being that it is
A language soft and sweet on the palate?

I declare English,
The language of the nation,
Is important for us to speak
And thus, it should be taught
And we not be left bereft of it.

But, this should not cause us
To not practice that language of Cervantes.

How can it be, gentlemen?
By what means will the native Mexican
Learn this foreign tongue?

Oh, they say, "teachers will come"
And they will teach English, German, and French
And all the languages.

These things I see as folly,
Turning round and round in the sky.

Now, how will the heart make sense of this
And be able to feel another living tongue?
Though easy to grasp,
To truly comprehend a language,
One must study and learn it,
But if it's plopped down,
How in heaven's name will one get it?

Still, today most of the people
Speak the Spanish language
And hold on to its legacy.
Let's insist on keeping our inheritance alive.

We will forever speak our
Ancient tongue
May it live long in our hearts.

I repeat, I see no reason
To leave it behind
Let it shine in the constitution,
Of the new proposed state of the union.

When the Mexican understands
The maternal tongue
It will be easy for him to learn
The language of the government.

We beseech the heavens,
Grant us understanding
And grant us the day when
We are able to speak English.

Gentlemen, it is only just
That we learn to speak it
And always reserve a place
For the language of the nation.

It's just and reasonable
But, I wish to remind you
That paying homage to Saint Paul
Does not disgrace Saint Peter.

Today, we Mexican teachers lag behind
As so few of our fellow countrymen
Received teaching credentials.
Remember that we have been formed
In the Spanish language.
Might it not improve things,
If we are concerned with equal rights,
That at the time for examination
We test in both Spanish and English?

As all agree that it is of paramount interest
That both Spanish and English
Reign together on American soil.

24. "Young Girls with No Choice but to Take On Anglo Ways," Mefistófeles (pseudonym)

El Independiente, vol. 4, no. 1, 20 March 1897,
Las Vegas, New Mexico

25. "Anglo-Hispanic Vervoritis: An Epidemic," Fray Tijeras (pseudonym)

El Nuevo Mexicano, vol. 29, no. 7,
30 August 1917, Santa Fe, New Mexico

26. "The Importance of the Spanish Language: A Speech Delivered by Miss Isabel Córdova in Trinidad, Colorado," Isabel Córdova

El Nuevo Mexicano, vol. 28, no. 3,
3 August 1916, Santa Fe, New Mexico

Lexical borrowing between language groups is a common sociolinguistic occurrence that happens when words from one language are introduced into another and when the daily use of borrowed terms (spoken or written) emerges in common exchange, either by choice or imposition. Sociolinguistic researchers confirm that lexical borrowing has a long history in New Mexico and adjoining regions where Spanish was the common language before the arrival of English speakers in mass numbers. A sustained and deep contact between Spanish and English produced changes in both directions. For example, an abundance of terms related to ranching and cowboy culture in English (e.g., *buckaroo, corral, lasso, rodeo, chaps, hoosegow,* etc.) are derived from Spanish terms.

Somewhere in the middle of the territorial period, the balance of exchange tilted decidedly, as Anglo-American influence in all social domains began to overpower the cultural capital of treaty citizens and, by extension, to fuel unease that the Spanish language was being eroded by the increasing dominance of English in public life. The greatest remonstrance on the part of Nuevomexicanos (the social group facing linguistic loss) was reserved for instances of the mixing of languages, or what contemporary sociolinguistics call "code-switching."

Nuevomexicanos came to understand that the resulting imbalance was exacerbated by value judgments that superseded the neutral exchange of terms. Language use came to be equated with an individual's social standing, and some measure of that standing was enforced through doctrines of prestige and denigration that prescribed which language was deemed acceptable (read: educated, normative, proper, official) and which language would be marked as defective, substandard, or foreign.

Decisions concerning which language was acceptable could determine one's place in society and a sense of which social standing one could aspire to reach. Conversely, in psychological terms, a person sought to be accorded respect as a measure of good repute. Anomalies and departures from expected language norms produced confusion through unintended incongruency or rote mimicry. Often, linguistic faux pas were treated humorously and were even parodied and ridiculed by those wishing to deride the perceived linguistic incompetency or deficiency of others.

The first two entries in this cluster present situations where the mixing of English and Spanish produces hilarious results. Many times, language was a vehicle to project self-importance or grandiosity—for example, when speakers with some degree of familiarity with English, the prestige language, engaged in a display of their supposed command of the language to elevate their standing and derisively mock others.

The first entry is a humorous *coloquio,* or dialogue, between a mother and daughter as they discuss the young lady's new love interest and her prior relationship with an Anglo man. At issue are the cultural differences between Nuevomexicano and Anglo social norms. The daughter's speech is liberally sprinkled with English, a habit encouraged by her mother, who attempts to speak in the same way. Here the use of English signals the speakers' desire to appear fashionable, in vogue, and to convince others that they are abreast of current trends.

We learn that, at her mother's insistence, the daughter looks to improve her chances at getting a new suitor to take her out on a date. The author of "Las agringadas por fuerza" ("Young Girls with No Choice but to Take On Anglo Ways") adds a twist to the story when it becomes known that the suitor is not an Anglo but a Mexican, a man of means who has come up to New Mexico from Mexico City. With irony the writer provokes readers by insinuating that the better option for the daughter would be to improve her Spanish and not her English in order to win over her suitor.

The second entry, "Anglo-hispano vervoritis: Una epidemia" ("Anglo-Hispanic Vervoritis: An Epidemic"),[74] is another example of a *décima,* in this case one issued by an invented persona, Fray Tijeras ("Friar Scissors"). The verses address the virtual epidemic of English words, or anglicisms, that are working their way into the daily speech of treaty citizens. The contagion, as Fray Tijeras notes, confounds and disrupts the older, accepted, and predictable language decorum. The offering is meant to produce humor in listeners at hearing the oscillating cadence of English and Spanish as words from one language bump into words from the other. The jocularity is amplified when words from the English and the Spanish collide as a series of mispronunciations that occasion laughter and jeers.

While questions of language could result in humorous evocations, as in the cases above, treaty citizens were deeply disturbed by the social conditions that threatened to separate them from their language. The third entry in this cluster, "La importancia del idioma español" ("The Importance of the Spanish Language"), is an insightful essay on the future of Spanish in the region, written by Isabel Córdova, a teacher in the early grades in Trinidad, Colorado (a bastion of treaty citizens). Information on Córdova is scant, though an accompanying editor's note introducing the piece to the readers of *El Nuevo Mexicano* informs us that Córdova is a member of a well-established family and a granddaughter of Rafael Chacón (entry 18). Her family background, as the editor suggests, credentials Córdova to speak on behalf of Nuevomexicanos in southern Colorado and northern New Mexico. The transcript of Córdova's speech, given to the Sacred Heart Society at a local Trinidad parish, appears to be her only contribution to Spanish-language newspapers. Other treaty citizens had addressed several of the concerns Córdova sets forth in her essay—most notably Aurora Lucero, whose essay "Shall the Spanish Language Be Taught in the Public Schools of New Mexico?" was selected as the winning essay in an oratorical contest sponsored by the New Mexico Normal University in Las Vegas, New Mexico, and was published in the *Normal University Bulletin* in 1911, on the eve of New Mexico's statehood. Lucero was the daughter of the prominent politician and journalist Antonio Lucero (entry 17). In her defense of the language, Aurora employs modern linguistic analysis, demographic data, and historical and cultural reasoning to insist on the social benefits that can result from an appreciation rather than a denigration of the Spanish language.

Coincidentally, Córdova and Lucero both base their defense of Spanish on similar reasoning. They argue that Spanish is the single most important aspect that defines the identity of their community. Both emphasize the noble and lyrical properties of Spanish and underscore the demographic importance of Spanish in the Western Hemisphere and in the world. Both signal its potential to improve commerce between the United States and Latin America.

Córdova, however, draws directly from the close, daily contact she maintains with her students, the majority of whom come from Spanish-speaking homes. Her observations hint at the psychological scarring she sees manifesting in students who express shame when asked to speak in their native language. A deep concern for the educational welfare and future development of these children drives Córdova's examination of how privileging English over Spanish is harmful to the minds of these children. For more on Spanish in the United States, see Lozano. For the particularities of lexical borrowing and code-switching, see García-Caba.

Works Cited

García-Caba, Marta. "Ni castellano, ni inglés, ni yankee, aquello es simplemente mexicano ayankado: La prensa fronteriza de finales del XIX como espacio para la construcción de una identidad sociolingüística." *Tempus Volat, AJIHLE MANET, Asociación de Jóvenes Investigadores en Historiografía y Historia de la Lengua Española*, coordinated by Ana María Romera Manzanares et al., Editorial Universidad de Sevilla, 2021, pp. 77–94.

Lozano, Rosina. *An American Language: The History of Spanish in the United States.* U of California P, 2018.

Lucero, Aurora. "Shall the Spanish Language Be Taught in the Public Schools of New Mexico?" *Normal University Bulletin*, no. 23, Jan. 1911.

Young Girls with No Choice but to Take On Anglo Ways

"Mom, *you know*[75] that Mexican that came from Mexico? He's making me sick to my stomach."

"But how so, my daughter? *What's the matter?*"

"*You know*, Mom, *he loves me*, but it's been three days since he's come to take me out walking, *you know.*"

"It's true that I knew he cared for you, and this is good for us since he's rich, and I trusted him and I let him come in the house and I gave him permission to go out with you in keeping with our American style, and it's hard for me to believe that he is not coming by for you in person."

"Yes, Mom, very hard, *that's true*, but get hold of him to see if he also finds it hard. We should demand he live up his responsibility, *you know.*"

"*Alright*, I'll have him come over, and he can't be fooling both of us. But if he comes by, I'm going to let him know what I've heard about him."

"*What, what?* Mom, *you make me sick.*"

"I heard he is always over at the Bravemore house and that he also takes those girls out to walk and that he doesn't return until midnight or one o'clock in morning."

"*Is that so?* I believe that's why I never liked those gals. *I hate e'm.* They're women, hussies, *you know.* I never talk to them. I do, *yes*, say hi to *Joe*, but them, *never.*"

"Well, you know I detest them, of course. With *Joe, that's different*. He's a sweet guy. And I bet what they like about your boyfriend is his big whiskers and his big nose in between them."

"*I don't know, Mom, about that.*"

"You don't know? *Patillas* is *whiskers*."

"*Oh, yes, I remember,* and I bet if they got the chance, they grabbed them and his nose as well. *Oooh! Jealous, that makes me sick, you know.*"

"*Well, well.* I'm going to have him come over. In the meantime, tell me the truth. How have you behaved when you have gone out with him? Don't keep anything from me because I know everything."

"Ah, Mom, *you frighten me, don't be so, you know.* The first time we went out, he seemed very polite, and I didn't understand everything he was telling me in Mexican. *The second time, you know.* He behaved more *lovely,* and he proposed many lovely things that I liked *very much.* Which was good 'cause I don't like Mexican politics. The third time he left me very enchanted and satisfied because he left me well put together, *you know.*"

"Daughter, you mean to say, he courted you well? Don't be so flighty."

"Oh, Mom, *I mean,* he made good love to me. *I don't know about la corte. I don't like that.* He has never taken me to court, *you know.*"

"Go on, go on, *fool, I won't get in a fight with you.* I'm going to have that Mexican from Mexico City come over because, you know what? This is also making me sick to my stomach. Go on, get dressed and put on some makeup so you're easier on his eyes and look better than how you look now. But first, puff up the armchairs and dust off everything because things are ugly with so much dust and filth, *ain't it?"*

"That's all right, Mom."

Next thing, the girl can be heard singing that black folks' song:[76]

I want yer, me honey, yes,
I want yer, mighty badly . . .

Anglo-Hispanic Vervoritis

Among our fellow citizens,
Those arriving from over there
And have lived some years
In this blessed land,
A rare disease has started to propagate,
And its terrible effects
Are accentuated
In certain individuals
Who run in *high life*[77] circles.

Said epidemic,
(and clear it's now an epidemic)
Starts to show itself,
In the clumsy habit
Of chewing gum or tobacco
In American *estáil* [style].

Then the presumed patient
Feeling like a Mister Taft,[78]
Replies to everything with a *yes*
and constantly asks *what?*
Never forgetting to ask *savvy?*
Or the well-known *all right!*

Another alarming symptom
Is lopping off the *mostách* [mustache]
Or the Chaplin-like cut
And from the same source,
Another novelty
The military haircut
In the pure style of the nation:
Half a head shaved clean,
The other half unkempt.

And thus, the sickness
Advances step-by-step
Until a fever for dancing sets in,
A deadly automatic shaking
That I'd label mechanical-dance-mania:
That macabre cancan,
A pit where style and morals sink low.

This constitutes phase one,
And phase two it's clear

As with any epidemic
Looks to be more dire.
The victim's speech changes
With *what*, and *good morning*
Piling up, but moored in place
Until a total bilingual mixture sets in
Which in fact reminds me
Of the speeches of that famous Chin-Chun-Chan.[79]

And to those who think
I'm speaking out of turn,
I copy here the following exchanges
Taken from real life.

—Are you sure you love me? *Savvy?*
—*Yes? You bet your life, and do you love me too?*
—*Sure!* You know well I do.
—*Well, alright! Tomorrow*, I'll talk to your father
And on October, *the twenty-sixth*
Even if your mother isn't for it
We'll get hitched *anyhow.*

Keep it in mind, Mary Louise,
that we'll go into town
(the center of town)
I want to take you to *Bullos*[80]
A very *smart* store,

You know that all this *week*,
There's a special sale.

—How do you like your Los Angeles?
It's a paradise, isn't it true?
—How do you know how I like them?
If I haven't mentioned this. Ah!
Now I understand,
You're talking to me
As is done around here;
You are translating literally from English
How do you like?
But man, and with you being a lawyer
With so much talent
To hear you say such barbarisms!
—I'm nervous, *chises cráis* [Jesus Christ]!

And all dribbled in,
With the *marketa* [market] and the *shop*.
The *telefón* [telephone] and the *watter* [restroom]

The *aromovil* [automobile] and the *raid* [ride]
The *moro saico* [motorcycle] and the *rueda* [bicycle]
The *bill* and the *San Abagán* [son of a gun]
And other lesser saints
Whose names I won't repeat,
These are all found in phase two
Of this deadly illness
Which is causing more harm
Than a German submarine.[81]

Hey, but I'm working
On a special antidote
To extinguish that microbe,
And I'll do it *anyhow.*
Dammit! I, too, am
Becoming infected;
And like the good judge
Who always starts his work at home
I'm going to take the first antidote
And bid you all *goodbye.*

The Importance of the Spanish Language

It is with true pride that we publish the following speech on the Spanish language and its importance, recently delivered by a young Hispanic-American woman before the Sacred Heart of Jesus Society in the town of Trinidad, Colorado. Miss Córdova is the daughter of Mister Carpio Córdova and Mrs. Gumercinada Chacón de Córdova and the granddaughter of Major Rafael Chacón and his wife. All are persons who reside in Trinidad and who are widely and favorably known, not only in the neighboring state to the north but also in New Mexico.

—A note from the editors

Reverend Fathers, Members of the Society of the Sacred Heart of Jesus, Ladies and Gentlemen:

As I stand before you to speak on the importance of the Spanish language, I cannot but recognize my limited capacity to speak on a subject as vast as this one is. I would have preferred that this task be assigned to a more capable person with greater experience than I, a person who would be able to infuse into your hearts a true love of our language and who could imprint on your thinking its importance.

The Castilian tongue is one of the most beautiful and refined among the neo-Latin, or Romance, languages, as they are called. In looking into its origins, we will find that it was formed across the course of centuries by the slow decomposition of Latin, and it had its beginnings and developed in the central and southern regions of Spain. History tells us that it came to be called Castilian since it was the most extensive and widely spoken of the languages in the vast area of Castile in the thirteenth, fourteenth, and fifteenth centuries, at a time when Castile comprised all territories of Spain, beyond those included under the crowns of Aragon, Portugal, and Navarra, and that it continued to be called by that name since no other could be had by which to set it apart, and being that it was as incorrect as calling it Spanish, a name that foreigners applied to the language at a later time.

There are no documents that can help us understand the day-to-day process of transformation that vulgar Latin took until it became Castilian in the twelfth century, the oldest form of the language that we are aware of, and even if these documents existed, it would be impossible to precisely fix the moment when Latin ceased to be Latin and began to be Castilian, and this happened on account of the gradual manner of this evolution, making it difficult to say when the change happened.

It is also impossible for there to be writing that in every case follows the process of development for every language, because all languages advance gradually—which is to say, through a period of gestation from an embryonic stage of life.

Castilian has been transmitted to us, with modifications, no doubt, as there is not a living language that does not continue to vary and modify itself as time goes on, up to the point of changing where they turn into other languages that are distinct, and this, too, is an unescapable law of nature. These modifications go much deeper in the case of the verbal forms of a language than in written forms, since there is no one to guard against the former, whereas in the case of the latter, grammar, instruction, and the intellectual culture of those who make use of the language guard against change.

There are many people who doubt that Spanish needs to be studied, since it appears to them that the spoken use of the language is sufficient. Let me give you a few examples:

Over the last four years I have been responsible for teaching the Spanish classes in this city. In these classes I have had in the sixth, seventh, and eighth grades an average of four hundred children each year, and of this number, about five percent have been Spanish speakers. Almost every year at the start of the term, some Mexican children asked to be excused from these classes, saying that they already know how to speak Spanish, and they say their parents tell them that it would be better for them to spend this time in some other useful activity.

It makes no difference how much Spanish they know; the district rules don't excuse them from these classes. Can we really think that learning the language is so little a concern for the majority of our children?

It is a very sad matter for me when at the end of each month I correct the exams and find that the American children end up with better grades than the Mexican children. It's very regrettable that they do not seem to want to take advantage of the opportunity.

In my visits to different schools, I have come upon children who are ashamed of their language. They refuse to speak Spanish, and when spoken to, they respond in English: "I don't understand what you are saying." Sometimes I run into children that all together don't know a single word of Spanish. These are children of Mexican parents, children who don't have a drop of foreign blood in them. Isn't this very sad?

Many times I have spoken to these children concerning the importance of their language. It's not enough to know the need and usefulness of speaking it, but it is also necessary for us to understand that we need to speak it with perfection.

When we study grammar, we can do no less than find that we learn new things. Sometimes we can corroborate points by applying the principles and foundations in our ordinary use of the language, and at other times we will find our many deficiencies will find correction. Grammar allows us to see the marvelous structure of the language, teaching us its parts, what its nouns are, their definitions and usage, and how sentences are woven together.

We don't think about such things before we are aware of the language arts, but that is difficult to do if we don't speak with precision.

It would be a great thing if the parents could instruct their children in the grammar of their language or, if they are not able to do this, see to it that the children get this kind of instruction. Were they to do this, they would see the advantages these children would have over others who can't express themselves in speech and writing.

There is no career or profession in which grammar does not prove useful. A famous rhetorician has said it is required in the children, pleasing to old people, a sweet companion in solitude, and, of all the fields of study, the one that offers the biggest challenges and much enlightenment.

We all know that English is the language of this country, and in order to live well and carry out our business with ease, it is necessary to know English, and this is why everyone pushes themselves to learn it and have their children learn it, so that in this way, they can acquire at least some amount of education. This must be acquired in English as the common language of the United

States. But the mothers and fathers should not allow their children to forget their language in order to learn the foreign tongue. Yes, it's good that they learn English. It's a must, but it is more necessary to learn their language, to learn it well, and to preserve it.

There is nothing stranger than to hear the boys and girls of today talking. Perhaps you have not thought about this, but take a listen and you'll see that it's nearly impossible to follow their conversation to the end. A word in English is said, and another in Spanish. If the thread of the conversation continues in this manner, in the end, English is not being spoken, nor is it Spanish, because the two languages are being mixed. If there happens to be a person who does not know either language, that person is left to fend for themselves.

Our youth are so accustomed to this style of conversation that it is impossible for them to avoid it. Some days ago, in a gathering of some Mexican ladies, it was suggested that they should speak only in Spanish since there was one lady who did not speak English, and since all the ladies were Mexican, this was only right and just. But being so used to mixing the two languages, they could not but veer from the decision. They imposed a fine of one penny for each word that was used in English. Some of the ladies decided it was best to stay quiet rather than risk being fined. In the end the fine had to be done away with, because they were not happy, and so that they could enjoy themselves, the whole idea was put aside, as happens. This was in the spirit of a dare, and we all took it as a dare, but it was a regrettable discovery for me. This shows what little interest and little appreciation we have for our own language.

If the parents required their children to speak Spanish and wouldn't permit them to mix the languages at home, I believe that in no time at all the children would become accustomed to speaking well.

In passing I cannot but praise the merits of such a sublime language; in poetry there is no other language that equals it in beauty and nobility; there is no other language as melodious.

The need for Spanish is real. It's required, and fairness demands that it be employed. We have the inspiring proof of this in the Quixote, a book that has been translated into every language to propagate as sweet harmony all that is grand and beautiful in literature.

Who is there who cannot admire the achievement of Cervantes in that immortal work? Who cannot but admire its lexicon, so accessible to everyone.

Spanish literature abounds with great works. How many of our young people know them? Very few. Some because they don't know how to read in Spanish, others because it is of little interest to familiarize themselves with them. The works of Cervantes, Lope de Vega, Calderón,[82] and many more have been translated into English because literary-minded people in the United States want to know the grandeur of Spanish literature.

In regard to commercial exchange, the road between this country and the republics of South and Central America, where Spanish is the national language, has been open for some time now. The demands of commerce make knowledge of Spanish a requirement.

Those Europeans who have settled in Mexico and in the Spanish Americas have acquired the habits of those countries along with the language. They speak and write it with fluency. Many of them have made great fortunes, and they have gained the political influence and trust of those people.

For the young people who are about to run the race of life, these examples should be very instructive; they will find that the foreigners are learning our language to be able to occupy available posts that require some measure of Castilian.

At present there is a great demand for young, educated people who can speak and write Spanish well.

There are positions as teachers, telegraph operators, accountants, and many others that are open, and not just in Spanish-speaking countries but also in the United States.

Why, then, should we let the foreigners get ahead of us, learn our language, and occupy these jobs and leave us behind?

Knowing the advantages that come from knowing Spanish, a great clamor has come forth across the country for its instruction in the schools. In the past it was taught only in colleges, then it was extended to high school, and now there is a great demand for it to be introduced into the lower grades of the schools in some communities.

In conclusion, I ask you, fathers and mothers, to reclaim Spanish as your own language and that you not forget your duty to transmit it to your children. We should have great pride in our glorious achievements and the merits of our nationality, of which there are many. May you pass news of these achievements from one hand to the next as the lamp that is to burn and shine the eternal flame, the spirit, and the life of the Spanish language.

27. "Upon Returning to This Piece of Earth: Ode to the City of Santa Fe," anonymous

La Revista Ilustrada, vol. 12, no. 11,
July-August 1925, Santa Fe, New Mexico

The anonymous poem "De regreso al terruño" ("Upon Returning to This Piece of Earth") appears to have come from a longtime subscriber to or someone closely associated with Santa Fe's *Revista Ilustrada* (*Illustrated Review*). As with Pero Grullo, the pseudonymous author of entry 29, several signs of erudition suggest that this author had some degree of training in letters. The poem consists of eleven-syllable lines set into four-line stanzas known as *cuartetos* (quatrains) and is another example of an *octava real* with higher-order versification and consonantal rhyme, as prescribed by *arte mayor* tradition. The poet's formal training is confirmed midway through the poem, when he invokes Homer and Dante in order to elevate this tribute to Santa Fe.

Camilo Padilla published his magazine, *Revista Ilustrada*, as a monthly for twenty-six years. The publication was contemporaneous with the New Mexico Historical Society's *El Palacio* and was born of the need Nuevomexicanos had for an analogous venue to feature their art and literature in their own language. From the start, the monthly created a previously unknown space for representing the creative work of treaty citizens. As a literary magazine, the publication featured poems, short stories, and historical writing. Each issue was illustrated with photographs, woodblock prints, and other graphics. As noted in entry 6, Padilla routinely opened his publication to submissions from his readership, and it was not unusual to find the work of widely published Latin American writers alongside that of Mexican American writers in a single issue.

Several individuals in north-central New Mexico possessed the skills needed to write this ode to the homeland. It is conceivable that this piece came from the pen of Camilo Padilla, who, as an economic migrant, shared the experience of having to leave his native Santa Fe on multiple occasions (see entry 7). Padilla spoke about his displacement in his short fiction, expressing a deeply felt *querencia*, or longing. In those moments he was apt to think that it was fate alone that had taken him away from his homeland. For more on Padilla, see Meléndez 69–72, 154–58. For more on Padilla's Centro de Cultura (Center for Culture), see Meléndez 197–99.

Work Cited

Meléndez, A. Gabriel. *So All Is Not Lost: The Poetics of Print in Nuevomexicano Communities, 1834–1958.* U of New Mexico P, 1997.

Upon Returning to This Piece of Earth

Oh, city of the holy faith of Saint Francis,
I sing to your fauna and winter gardens
That evoke the grace and beauty,
Nature has lavished on you.

I sing to the soft breezes,
And the grace of your lovely flowers and songbirds
And where the beautiful woman,
The goddess of this sanctuary is caressed.

Allow me to offer my love to you,
A love you inspired in me from childhood,
May this heart of mine rejoice,
And look upon your beauty eternally.

You are a striking princess,
A worthy muse for Homer and Dante Alighieri
Who surely would have found inspiration in your
    grandeur
In your noble grace and talents.

Your fountains, your birds, and your flowers
Are a wedding bed for all lovers,
And the hope of peace for one
Who has only known pain and malice.

Your four hundred years of life
Have been filled with goodness drawn from deep
    experience,
These are the things you leave to counsel your children,
The sage lessons of long experience.

And you greet all those you meet at dawn,
With the grace of a sovereign Virgin
So that they can hold up their heads
As they face the difficult battles of this current age.

I, one of your children,

traverse a sad and long road,

And see the frost of life,

Drop down on this, my beloved pathway.

I return to you, my chest now full,

With good fortune and pleasures,

With your lips, the lips of a mother

You have spoken "Go forward,"

To all like me who have tasted bitter wine.

Oh, blessed earth, if only there were something

to transform this fleeting life,

Into an everlasting springtime

So that hope would always endure without end.

And that I could live thinking only

Of the bliss and good fortune,

Though passing things,

leaving only their wake in this life

Like a memory of a lost dream.

May you be the lady of my soul

And the bright dawn of my life

That I may sing forever,

The glories of your past and your present.

28. "The Humble Home," Luz Elena Ortiz

La Revista Ilustrada, vol. 12, no. 12,
September 1925, Santa Fe, New Mexico

La Revista Ilustrada (*The Illustrated Review*) welcomed and
published contributions from male and female subscrib-
ers such as "El humilde hogar" ("The Humble Home"),
written by the Santa Fe resident Luz Elena Ortiz. Little is
known about Ortiz, making her contribution to Camilo Pa-
dilla's literary magazine noteworthy, since it represents an
early and infrequent example of a woman writing on social
topics and signing her work. It is probable that Ortiz drew
on the prominence of her family name. The Ortizes were a
well-known and highly regarded clan in and around Santa
Fe. It is also likely that Ortiz herself was educated at Santa
Fe's Loretto Academia, a parochial school that catered to
such families. She may have also been an early supporter
and an affiliate of El Centro de Cultura (The Center for Cul-
ture), a center founded by Padilla as a public forum for the
expression of Nuevomexicano art and culture. The piece is
a novel, passionate, and sustained critique of the social con-
ditions negatively affecting treaty citizens. For residents of
Santa Fe with roots going back to the 1692 repopulation of
Santa Fe by Diego de Vargas, the acceleration of moderniz-
ing trends would have deleterious effects for the natives of
New Mexico. Ortiz asserts the interests of the old families
of Santa Fe were routinely dismissed even as statehood had
promised to accord to them equal standing in their home
community. Ortiz not only points out how treaty citizens
are badgered and forced to assimilate culturally, she is also
aware that they are being forced to sell their lands and join
the laboring classes to gain their livelihood.

Oritz writes of the economically and socially disadvan-
taged condition of her Nuevomexicano neighbors, whose
lifestyle is very different from that of an elite group of re-
cent transplants to Santa Fe. She begins with observations

of the home environment, where the simple mud-plastered adobe houses that surround her, lacking modern amenities, stand in stark contrast to the ostentatious displays of affluence and privilege found in a growing number of Anglo-American enclaves in the city. She goes on to list the work available to tradesmen and laborers in her community. In the toils and travails of the common man (the sailor, the miner, the soldier, and the farmer), she sees dignity and nobility.

At several points, Ortiz quite unabashedly sublimates woman as maternal figure to the stature of a near deity. Partly, this comparative evocation unites motherhood with Catholic teachings on Marianism. Paul Horgan observes a generalized fascination with the matriarch in Nuevomexicano society of the 1920s, which he reasons grew out of long-held traditions of rich and poor families in Santa Fe. Horgan could easily be speaking of Ortiz's "The Humble Home" when he remarks, "In a superb indifference to any essential change the matriarch's descendants conduct themselves as though Santa Fe still belonged to them" (338). The burden imposed by newcomers was a heavy one for a people who had been accustomed to governing their own affairs with relative autonomy, the price Santa Fe's native residents were required to pay in the name of progress, according to Ortiz.

Readers of *Revista Ilustrada* appreciated Ortiz's remarks, as demonstrated by the compliments paid to the piece by a subscriber, Benigno Padilla, in a follow-up issue. Padilla says that he read Ortiz's article with interest and agrees with her that the people of New Mexico faced deplorable social conditions and that it was the duty of the Spanish-language journalist to defend the community. For more on Ortiz, see Meléndez 195, 197, 205–06.

Works Cited

Horgan, Paul. *The Centuries of Santa Fe.* U of New Mexico P, 1984.

Meléndez, A. Gabriel. *So All Is Not Lost: The Poetics of Print in Nuevomexicano Communities, 1834–1958.* U of New Mexico P, 1997.

Padilla, Benigno. "Lo que más necesitamos." *La Revista Ilustrada*, vol. 13, no. 2, Sept. 1925, p. 4.

The Humble Home

Home filled with memories,
I so want to return to you,
There is no other place under the sun
As sweet as one's home
I might be found in a palace
Circling the globe,
But, of all places, I prefer
My home, sweet home.

I don't know who provided us with the beautiful translation of a song now known to all the world and which heads up my humble and sincere tribute to what is "the parlor of the world," as they say in English when speaking of the most useful and needed thing for human well-being. Why do I list the farmer as the most needed person for us? Is it not the dizzying luxury of the "multimillionaire's" home that is to be most admired and talked about? How can I dare to go against the current and the present order of things? Isn't it the case that medical doctors are equally praised and raised up in stature? And they are to be seen as the most deserving to be followed and at all costs. Those poor folk who steal a cow out of great need or hunger and to feed their young ones or the elders they care for are sent to the penitentiary to expunge their "vile crime."

Those that amass vast sums of money, if at the cost of the lives of others, are honored and called benefactors. They are acclaimed as the best examples of the human race. Why? We ask again.

In a simple hut everything is made by the great work and sweat of the owners. There the floors are not paved with marble or fine woods. The place is cold, not having carpet or tapestry. On winter nights the wind whistles everywhere. In an opposite scene, the "last word" in vanity and fashion reigns. There the god of all things modern, like the ancient idol of the golden calf, is worshiped.

They say that the feminine sex always has anarchistic tendencies, but these would be better called socialistic inclinations. It could be that at times women see things more clearly, gifted as they are with a sixth sense, which is called instinct in irrational animals. Or, better yet, it could be that they admire the strong spirit of the poor, above all that of the mother of the family. Mothers have always had my admiration, respect, and love wherever they are to be found.

Oh, mother, a holy name across the whole of the earth. What can fathers accomplish—although they be golden men—where the woman's presence is absent from the home? Even in the home of the poor, in a crude house made from earth, a house made by hand, there is a holy altar dedicated to you. There, the mother, surrounded by her children, is worshiped. For she looks after them, protects them, and guards them day and night, even when sleep defeats the strongest workman. They find warmth in her arms and protection from all harm when darkness grows in the evening and sleep pulls down the eyelids. Here is an ideal that even the most brilliant and gifted mind can fully embrace. Cold, empty, and without feeling are those words, but the home is always where the mother resides. Where she is most nobly appreciated.

There, the light of the sky,
Descends most serenely,
Filled with a thousand delights,
The home is a blessing,
Where the hours fly by
In moments so brief and so joyous
There, all things
Can be cherished continually.

A man will retrace his steps and his thoughts at the end of each day and be brought back to the home. And yet, the fashionable will ask, what joy can be had in a mud hut? What is "comfortable"[83] about it? The man's wife always keeps a fire going and prepares meals and brings peace. The bigger the family, the greater the subtleness of the love therein: wife, children, and elderly parents.

I ask, what can be found in the most elegant mansion, in the richest palace, where no peace, harmony, or love is present? Might it be that these three words mesh and join in a single name, when a man chooses his life companion well? Even the beast of the forest has a cave where it takes refuge at night, away from predators. But what does it have if it does not have tranquility at the end of the continual struggle for survival? His enemies control him, and while they could provide peace, the beast is hunted. That animal, the king of the mountains, lacks what the real lion has in his home. "Man is made to seek adventure, not so the woman" is often repeated by farm women, who prefer the tasks of their home to any form of feminist emancipation.

Out on the vast ocean, the sailor generously faces the dangers of an array of unchained natural elements. Hurricanes blow and whip his fragile ship, the sea roars, lightning lights up the profound darkness around him, rain falls in torrents and threatens to drown him in the abyss. And amid all the danger and across the immense distance an idea, a sublime image, lights up his thinking. He has in his thoughts a memory that he keeps, and at that very moment, he sees his spouse, sad and alone, and he becomes aware of the dire future his children will face should the sea claim his arms that are now the shield and guardrail that provide for his children.

The miner, bereft of sun and light, nearly without air, amid the dark and freezing shadows of the mines, is always in danger. He "spends his life," if we can call it that, sacrificing the life of his home.

The soldier confronts an enemy who would kill him without mercy if he could; they both are innocent victims, often because of the ambition and power of others. Victim and victimizer, both could fall at the same moment, but they both carry the indelible image of their homes, their mothers, their wives, and perhaps their children in their thoughts.

The farmer carries on with his difficult work with equal purpose. The burning sun cannot make him collapse; the frigid wind does not scare him; the rain does not impede him; the spring wind does not hold him back. All things push him to toil more. His vivid imagination lights up, and he sees a faithful picture engraved in him forever of his home and children.

But is the Hispanic-American press asleep? Can't it see the danger? The time for political talk has passed. Does the poor subscriber have the right to expect that the press will write in her defense? So many good newspapers with strong circulation, so many talented writers in Spanish with clear talent and able pen who could lend themselves to write about the regrettable situation in which the poor people of our community find themselves, those who hold on to a few acres of land. Unity and harmony among the writers are much needed, more now than ever, given the dire condition in which the people of New Mexico find themselves. After being tossed out of their lands and homes, what can they do? They find themselves obligated to pave the public roadways for the benefit of others, since they seldom use them, unless it sometimes be by the poor donkey carrying the woodsmen's load. The automobile owner and the "tourist" expect that others will pay for those roads. Emigrate to other places? Why, and where? Let the foreigner acquire by unjust means the lands that have been held by their ancestors for two hundred years or more, ancestors who with sword in hand opened pathways through the hills, the forests, and enemies.

Dear gentlemen editors, the work is not about starting this defense, but rather to not halt the pen once it is in motion. The cause you are committed to is immense. It is sacred and magnificent. Go live among the poor as I have done by going to the smallest hamlets. Interact with the humble people, as they are called in this world. Speak to the ignorant, as the learned men from back East label them. Be a guide to them and their children. Do this and you will never forget them!

Poetry exists in the heart of the farmer. His seedlings, his trees, even the simple flowers that grace the inside and outside of his home. All these things he loves, and it breaks his heart to have to leave them and emigrate.

More than palaces,
To be enjoyed in a foreign land,
I wish to go back to my cabin,
My peaceful home.
There, the small birds,
Bring me joy with their songs,
There, with a thousand delights
shines the light of complete serenity.

VIII. On the Graves of Our Ancestors

29. "The Dawson Mine Catastrophe, 23 October 1913," Pero Grullo (pseudonym)

El Nuevo Mexicano, vol. 25, no. 17,
13 November 1913, Santa Fe, New Mexico[84]

"La catastrophe de Dawson" ("The Dawson Mine Catastrophe") is the work of an anonymous community poet who signed the piece with the widely used pseudonym "Pero Grullo,"[85] meaning "every person" or, more precisely, the kind of person given to stating the obvious. In the guise of a commoner, the "Pero Grullo" of these verses is actually a learned writer with enough skill to craft higher-order verses used by bards working in the *arte mayor* tradition. This "Pero Grullo" knows enough to render his lament in octosyllabic lines packed into eight-verse strophes, known as *octava reales*.

On 30 October 1913, *El Nuevo Mexicano* brought forth new details regarding the mine explosion that had occurred the week prior. Dawson, New Mexico, a Phelps Dodge mining town near the Colorado border, the paper noted, was the site of the worst mine disaster to have occurred in New Mexico up to that time. The paper reported that twenty-two miners had been rescued and that 284 men remained buried inside shafts 2 and 3 of the Dawson mine. Two weeks later, some verses in the form of a *corrido*, or ballad, memorializing the victims of a mining accident appeared in the paper. Pero Grullo's formal training did not distance him from the suffering at Dawson, where at least a third of the miners hailed from villages and towns in north-central New Mexico. The author's voice is strained with affect for the three hundred victims of the explosion and for the hundreds of relatives who experienced their loss.

The ballad progresses as if by drumbeat, becoming a procession of sorrow and loss. The opening stanzas heave ahead, burdened by the weight and scale of the catastrophe, growing in emotion to a crescendo at the middle stanzas and ebbing to a close with the dire realization that death acts mercifully when it takes away each of the surviving miners as they lie injured and near death on the train tracks. The totality of grief and sorrow is depicted as a troop of distraught mothers, widows, and orphaned children filing into the mining camp to look for their family members. Tragedy would visit the Dawson mining community ten years later, in 1923, when a second mine explosion killed another 120 miners. Nuevomexicanos were by this time more deeply enveloped in the wage-labor economy that steadily and over decades took them out of the villages and into jobs in mining, railroad, and agricultural in New Mexico, Colorado, Wyoming, and other parts of the West. No doubt, somewhere in New Mexico, community bards, sometimes trained or, most often, self-taught, composed other ballads to draw attention to that other mining disaster. The journalist and newspaper reporter Nick Pappas has written extensively about the two explosions at the Dawson mine.

Work Cited

Pappas, Nick. *Crosses of Iron: The Tragic Story of Dawson, New Mexico, and Its Twin Mining Disasters.* U of New Mexico P, 2023.

The Dawson Mine Catastrophe

Look upon so many wretched folk,

Feverously at work

Earning their living,
With sweat and toil,
Unaware, they did not fear the danger
Or thought it far off, somewhere
And then the explosion came
That killed all three hundred miners.

Three hundred miners there, employed
Nearly all of them are dead and gone
Very few have made it out alive.
Bodies lined up and placed in heaps,
There they lie and begin to bloat,
And when help finally arrives.
All that can be seen are the dead.

What a pitiful sight
Havoc and horror on display
All around the rotting remains
Of the many human beings
Who have succumbed to the gases
Or have been consumed by fire
It's all but certain that many
Were long in dying that day,
Only after a prolonged agony
Did they finally expire,
Rest being the only thing
That Death at last could give them.

After so many supplications
Crossed over their chests,
Suffering, clamored, shrieked,
And Death did finally hear
and mercifully appeared.

But, oh, the dead were not
The worst of it,
But the living, standing at the mine entrance
who cry out in laments
Parents, wives, sons, and daughters
Standing, too, are the friends and brothers
Of the many who perished.
They wait on news
Fearing all is lost,
In desperation they shriek their pleas
Calling to their loved ones,
But hear no sound or answer come
Only silence surrounds them,
Because, inside, the mine
Is now just one vast, common grave.

Oh! Poor wretched victims!
So blind at the coming of misfortune
Tragedy that has no remedy,
Pain can't be quelled.
So many unfortunate widows,

So many mothers weep

So absolute is this desertion,

And misery and destitution

Surrounds them.

Alone, helpless, destitute.

Their ill has no cure

No one can fully grasp it

Save for God in heaven above

Who comes to aid the lost and deserted.

30. "In Memory of Narciso Romero," anonymous

El Nuevo Mexicano, vol. 27, no. 33,
2 March 1916, Santa Fe, New Mexico

"En memoria de Narciso Romero" ("In Memory of Narciso Romero") functions as a micro-elegy meant to bring solace to bereaved families and communities. The text includes formulaic elements found in secular ballads, such as those employed in the *corrido* tradition. The verse maker employs versification and stanzas in the *arte menor*, or popular, tradition. The stanzas are *cuartetos* (quatrains), eight syllables in length with consonantal rhyme. As a service to their readership, Spanish-language newspapers routinely gave space to the publication of death notices called *defunciones*, the equivalent of contemporary obituaries. Readers themselves, however, often submitted verse memorials alone or as part of death notices. These verse tributes, which function as word monuments, were composed to honor neighbors and relatives and rely on oral forms that preceded the arrival of print culture in the Nue-vomexicano community.

Most of these tributes are the work of untutored members of the community. Many times, the composer is a close relative who grieves alongside other surviving family members. Verse memorials are the work of either male or female composers who follow the requirements prescribed by custom and oral recitation, drawing on customs of verse memorializing passed down through oral recitation and, especially, through the singing of ballads. As prescribed, the bard gives the name and age of the deceased, the date of death, the manner of death, the individual's position in life, and anything notable regarding the person's disposition in the days prior to their death. The closing stanza often mentions the composer's name and relationship to the deceased. Secular ballads, as scholars of the *corrido* tradition remind us, rely on similar formulaic rules, since prior to the appearance of print culture, they functioned as news reports.

The dramatic and emotive power of these word monuments intensifies in those stanzas reserved for the *despe-dida*, or farewell. It is at this point that the text's vantage point shifts to narrate events as if seen through the eyes of the deceased, causing an evocation of the most stirring sensations as the deceased appears to address the living. This stylistic trait is present in earlier texts: for instance, "El corrido de un cibolero" ("The Ballad of a Buffalo Hunter"; entry 4).

It is in the farewell that the bonds between the deceased and any number of family members or friends are reviewed, the degree of kinship determining the extent of the address offered to each person named. Other factors can trigger entreaties to those left behind, such as persons who witnessed the death or assisted during the illness or relatives entrusted with the care of the deceased's children.

Cases of unexpected death, such as the loss of infants and children, gave rise to especially moving verses. Death by accident, especially in youth, was the cause of great lamentation. In the verse memorial that follows, a young man, Narciso Romero, is accidentally shot by his cousin Blas Valdez as they are shooting targets. Two months after the accident, Santa Fe's *El Nuevo Mexicano* published the tribute. This word monument includes a distended *despedida* through which family, friends, and even the shooter take turns expressing their remorse given the enormity of the tragedy that befell this community of farmers and ranchers. Narciso's presence haunts the text as he addresses his executioner, Blas. As his beleaguered widow calls back to Narciso, "[s]e apretaba el corazón" ("her heart twisted into a knot"). For more on the oral tradition of verse memorializing in New Mexico, see Meléndez, "'Adios Acompañamiento'" and "Death Notices."

Works Cited

Meléndez, A. Gabriel. "'Adios Acompañamiento': Text and Context of a New Mexican Alabado." *Chicano Discourse: Selected Conference Proceedings of the National Association for Chicano Studies*, edited by Tatcho Mindiola, Jr., and Emilio Zamora, U of Houston, Mexican American Studies Program, 1992, pp. 105–15.

———. "Death Notices, Word Monuments and Funerary Verse-Memorializing in *El Nuevo Mexicano*, 1906 to 1920." *New Mexico Historical Review*, vol. 100, no. 1, winter 2025, forthcoming.

In Memory of Narciso Romero

I ask God's permission,

And may He refresh my memory,

As I pray for this deceased man

That God will take him up to glory.

In the year 1916

Oh, how I wish I could forget,

Young people, you must know
that rifles are known to kill.

Listen, and pay close attention,
And I shall tell you the story
So you, too, can pray for the deceased
That God will take him to glory.

Oh, what a tragedy has occurred
On the fourth of January
When Blas Valdez, who was shooting targets,
Killed Narciso Romero.

A tragedy indeed, as so happened,
May God help us understand it,
He was only twenty-six years old
On the day that he died.

Abrenio, he came running in
And said one man had been killed
My brother-in-law, Blas Valdez
Shot a bullet into my brother.

Poor Blas Valdez
The people will defame him,
Ignoring that this came about
As the result of a sad accident.

May God spread His consolation,
On the parents of the deceased
And also on Agapita,
Given the bad luck she has had.

The poor sister of Romero
There with her heart split in two
At the sight of her dead little brother
Dead by the hand of her husband.

Poor wretched parents of Blas
They did not know what to think
They shed many tears
For their dear son Blas.

And poor little orphans
The three children Narciso had
They are left without the father
Who had done everything for them.

Farewell, dear parents, the love of my life,
The jewels of my heart
I am leaving this world
Now, give me your final blessing.

The deceased had two brothers
And three grown, younger sisters

They wept at his absence,
For he will never return home.

Farewell, my sweet wife,
And also my beloved grandmother
Here, they remain weeping
Like wounded doves.

Farewell, dear parents, the love of my life
Now, my soul has taken flight
Farewell, my mother Manuelita,
And my father, Jesús Romero.

Farewell, dear husband,
Jewel of my heart
Between sobs, Agapita would call out
As her heart twisted into a knot.
[Note: These verses were incomplete upon arrival, and we have published only what we received.]

31. "In Memory of Governor E. C. de Baca, a Speech Delivered by Attorney Octaviano A. Larrazolo at the State Legislative Session Held on the Third Day of the Present Month," Octaviano A. Larrazolo

La Voz del Pueblo, vol. 29, no. 8, 17 March 1917,
Las Vegas, New Mexico

"En memoria del gobernador E. C. de Baca" ("In Memory of Governor E. C. de Baca") is the text of the eulogy, originally delivered in English, by Octaviano A. Larrazolo to the state legislature of New Mexico on the occasion of the death of Governor Ezequiel Cabeza de Baca. The speech was later published in Spanish in *La Voz del Pueblo* (*The Voice of the People*).

After 1912 treaty citizens continued to hope that their economic and political fortunes would improve. Statehood, they believed, would roll back the decades of their having been denied full participation in public life. It came as a deep blow to treaty citizens to learn that the first native son among them to be elected governor of New Mexico, Ezequiel Cabeza de Baca (1864–1917), died after only six weeks in office, having been forced by ill health to conduct the affairs of state from a room at St. Vincent's Hospital in Santa Fe. Cabeza de Baca's death made realists out of dreamers by bringing into view just how difficult it would be for Nuevomexicanos to take the helm of self-rule and self-government. Cabeza de Baca's passing was symbolic and consequential, providing the moment to lament his loss, extoll his merits, and take stock of the decades of struggle that had preceded his 1916 race for governor, the second term after statehood.

Mutual suspicion fueled by continuing social and cultural divisions between Anglos and Nuevomexicanos were often magnified at the occasion of key life events (birth, marriage, death, etc.), moments when communities fell back into their social enclaves to celebrate, grieve, honor, and pay tribute to members of their group in prescribed and habitual ways.

As expected, the task of eulogizing the governor fell to another leading Nuevomexicano politician, Octaviano A. Larrazolo (1859–1930). A gifted speaker, Larrazolo was often referred to as "the silver-tongued orator." By his day, silent film and sound recording had come to New Mexico, and there is some evidence that Larrazolo was filmed walking around the state capitol during the George Curry[86] administration. Regrettably, no voice recording of him has ever surfaced. Like most of the other texts in this collection, Larrazolo's eulogy for Cabeza de Baca was crafted as a speech that listeners could experience as a performance. The fact that Larrazolo's elegy was meant for a legislative session required that it be made in English. The fullest rendering of his tribute, however, would have been in Spanish, the mother tongue of both Cabeza de Baca and Larrazolo, and, as would be expected, the text was quickly published by the Spanish weekly *La Voz del Pueblo* of Las Vegas, New Mexico, soon after its delivery.

Larrazolo and Cabeza de Baca were brought together by politics and personal friendship. Larrazolo recalls that it was his good fortune to count the governor among the first friends he made when he moved to Las Vegas twenty-two years before, when, as Larrazolo notes, "él estaba en la flor de su juventud" ("he was in the flower of his youth"). The two shared an interest in politics. (Larrazolo would become New Mexico's fourth governor in 1919 and was elected to the US Senate in 1928.) Both were Catholics, Democrats, native speakers of Spanish, and part of large extended families. Larrazolo was not a native of New Mexico. Rather, he was a Mexican citizen who had been born in the state of Chihuahua and had left Mexico as a young man to pursue his education under the tutelage of Archbishop Jean-Baptiste Salpointe. Salpointe would eventually recruit Larrazolo to study at St. Michael's College in

Santa Fe, where the latter grew to understand the histori-
cal cause of New Mexico's treaty citizens, the majority of
whom were his classmates.

Larrazolo knew how much his Nuevomexicano neigh-
bors valued their history and heritage, and he seized on
the opportunity to extol such matters in the eulogy he
prepared for his departed friend. He manages to do this by
raising up Cabeza de Baca's family crest, partly imagined
and partly true, which he ties to the sixteenth-century ship-
wreck survivor Álvar Núñez Cabeza de Vaca. The castaway
and four other survivors had over the course of seven years
trekked across the continent from the Gulf of Mexico, skirt-
ing southern New Mexico and eventually rejoining with
other Europeans in northern Mexico in 1536.[87]

Larrazolo did not feel compelled to doubt family lore
and chose to draw on the symbolic power of the coinci-
dence of a family name to elevate Ezequiel and to ennoble
the role of treaty citizens in the history of the region. A
novelist, as Larrazolo insists in his paean, could not create
a more dramatic tale of romance and adventure than one
that linked Ezequiel to the figure and the trials of Alvar,
the ultimate protagonist in a tale of survival.

If, then, Alvar is the ultimate survivor, Larrazolo lik-
ens his trek to the wandering of the Israelites in the desert
and likewise to the Nuevomexicano cause for equal rights,
suggesting that having wandered for forty years through a
political desert, the Nuevomexicanos were finally "investi-
dos con una insignia de ciudadanía" ("invested with a sym-
bol of citizenship") and with the pride of seeing Cabeza de
Baca become New Mexico's second governor. For more on
Cabeza de Baca's contributions to the Spanish-language
press, see Meléndez 84–86. For more on Cabeza de Vaca,
see Reséndez 1–10. For information on the public life of
Larrazolo, see Gonzales 95–109.

Works Cited

Gonzales, Phillip B. "Race, Party, Class: The Contradictions
    of Octaviano Larrazolo." *Noble Purposes: Nine Champions*

of the Rule of Law, edited by Norman Gross, Ohio UP, 2007, pp. 95–109.

Meléndez, A. Gabriel. *So All Is Not Lost: The Poetics of Print in Nuevomexicano Communities, 1834–1958*. U of New Mexico P, 1997.

Reséndez, Andrés. *A Land So Strange: The Epic Journey of Cabeza de Vaca*. Basic Books, 2007.

In Memory of Governor E. C. de Baca

Your Excellency, Senators, Representatives, Honorable Judges, Ladies and Gentlemen:

It's a beautiful trait in human nature that despite whatever differences in our lives, no matter how much we may have differed from our fellow citizens in viewpoints and opinions, no matter how bitter and acrid our opposition to one another might have been in life, all these things are buried with the dead, and we love to dwell only on their virtues and good qualities. We love to raise up our sight and see them as an inspiration for others to follow and emulate.

In this very distinguished and respectable audience I see many who, like me, in an honorable and sincere way, differed with the viewpoints of the deceased governor, in whose memory we have gathered, and yet, we all stand ready to give a generous testimonial of our high appreciation of the pure values of his heart and his merits as a man. This explains why this distinguished group, headed by the chief executive and with the honorable members of both branches of the legislature and the honorable members of our state supreme court, has gathered on this solemn occasion.

Any intent to set down in a brief fashion the high points and the most interesting episodes in the life of the departed Governor Baca or the major traits of his character would be fruitless without first going over the earliest period in the history of the state, to which, by virtue of his genealogy, he is closely connected.

For the first descendent of a gallant and daring race who first dug at its earth and pointed the way to the founding of an empire in this part of the New World is he who was called by a free people to govern as the chief executive of the land of his ancestors. Ezequiel Cabeza de Baca brought together in his own brief life a good dose of the romance and tragedy that characterize the history of this race in its march over the centuries.

This is truly the case here. A novelist could never land upon a more appropriate theme to add beauty to his poetic pursuits than the figure of a weary traveler, torn and near defeat. He has been abandoned by companions and wanders across enemy beaches along the Gulf of Mexico. At points, he is chased and tormented by natives. He shoulders hardship, torture, and the humiliation brought on by seven years of captivity at the hands of a number of indigenous tribes living in this land. He finally manages to escape. His feet are lacerated, and he is hungry and thirsty, but he still exhibits an admirable resoluteness and an unbroken faith in Divine Providence; ever present, ever vigilant, it guides his steps. In 1536, while traversing unnavigable prairies and the inhospitable deserts of New Mexico, he seeks his brethren in the distant South. At last, Álvar Núñez Cabeza de Vaca manages to see himself among his own kind, who greet him as a prodigal son who returns home after such a long time. He points a prophetic finger at them and says, "There, then, is the route to the North, where lies an empire in the beautiful land of the Seven Cities of Cibola."[88]

The inspiring eloquence of Peter the Hermit,[89] in inflaming the spirit of conquest and adventure in the hearts of the Crusaders, was no greater than the words of Cabeza de Vaca to the brave sons of Castile and Aragon. For just look at the speed with which expeditions followed, one after another, to explore and conquer these lands. First came the always civilizing emblem of Christianity, the cross carried by Marcos de Niza in 1539. Then came the expedition of Agustín Ruíz in 1581. Espejo followed in 1582. Then came Castaño de Sosa in 1590, followed by Humana y Bonilla and, finally, Oñate,[90] who once and for all firmly established the influence of Christian civilization in a land where chaos had reigned supreme since time immemorial. And the struggle between the newly arrived and ancient owners of the land continued without letup over centuries, since it was not until Geronimo, the last of warrior chiefs, was subdued in 1886 that peace and security could be enjoyed in this land.

And all the while, the long and bloody battle by this people continued to redeem this land from wilderness. What were the political machinations of his countrymen? Sad is precisely the way to describe their history. Beautiful and mournful was their strength and their patience, resisting defeat like pawns placed on the spacious chessboard representing the politics of the world. They were tossed about by the hand of destiny from one condition to another, and not until very recently have they been able to enjoy the full measure of becoming free men. They successively knew the rule of kings, emperors, triumvirates,[91] military despots, and dictators and of the most humane and liberal institutions of this republic. Under such circumstances, however, they have always been true and loyal citizens of this remarkable land, which now the hand of Divine Providence has finally made a part of this country. They have proven again and again their loyalty and devotion to the government. They have done this by unselfishly shedding their blood and by depositing their lives in defense of the flag and have done all this, fixing their sight on the passage of time, waiting for the moment when the slow hand of time would point to the hour of their redemption. The hour finally came when on the sixth of January 1912, President Taft[92] signed a proclamation admitting New Mexico as a state of the union.

After wandering in the desert for forty years, the people of Israel were no happier when they saw the promised land than were the sons of New Mexico when they were invested with a symbol of citizenship, in equality with their fellow brothers in this nation of free men. After four centuries of patient waiting and struggle, in unison, they raised their hands to God in praise that their day of liberation had arrived.

Unlike other folks, they were unsure as to how they might proceed to canvass the entire state. How they might manage to find someone from their own fold, a descendent, if one could be had, of one of the first heroes to arrive here, the genesis of a magnificent legacy for us and our posterity. They looked for someone in whom to place the executive power of the state, someone they would be able to stand with near the graves of their ancestors and declare, "Look at how we, your sons, have been loyal to the faith you have deposited in us across countless generations in which we have bled and died. We have seen our sons fall into brutal captivity so that we might witness this day and be able to come and offer this proud result for your sacrifices and devotion. Here is this pure, upright, and capable descendent. The honor and true appreciation of his fellow citizens has called him to the executive post in the land you all conquered, which is today the home of the free and prosperous, of free and independent men."

The people sought and found their candidate in the beautiful Meadow City, nestled at the foothills of the Rocky Mountains. I knew him personally and intimately, as we were neighbors and friends. When the news of his nomination to this exalted post reached his hometown, his neighbors and fellow countrymen were completely overtaken with enthusiasm. Their joy knew no limits, and putting aside party affiliation and political differences, Republicans, Democrats, progressives, socialists, men, women, and children all rushed together as a mixed, undifferentiated group to honor and congratulate him for the much merited recognition that he had been accorded. This kind of public adulation had never before been seen in Las Vegas. It had been decreed by Divine Providence that once again, and not long after, the same tributes would be made to this beloved citizen on the occasion of his death.

I clearly recall that special day at the start of last September when a group of my friends picked me to speak and express our congratulations to this distinguished son of Las Vegas on that glorious occasion. Then, as now, in what I shall call an irony of fate, that group placed on me the sad duty of showing his virtues as a man, now upon his passing.

The task entrusted to me, in truth, is very sad for me but one that you, the honorable members of the legislature of the state, have considered me capable of carrying out and one that graciously has been asked of me is an honor that I do not merit and one that I will always hold close to me with sadness and, at the same time, in loving memory. It is a task my wife and children will always be proud of and for which they and I feel profoundly grateful to all of you.

Who was the man whose memory has united us here to honor him for all time, that son of New Mexico, the first to be called by the popular mandate of his people to assume the duties of the chief executive of the state?

We have seen that in 1536, Álvar Núñez Cabeza de Vaca was the man of the hour, and today it is Ezequiel Cabeza de Baca. This sounds like a novel, and yet it is a fact. Divine Providence is just in all its actions.

Now, my friends, I want to speak of how I came to know him, because it was indeed my good fortune to count him as one of the first friends I made when I arrived in Las Vegas some twenty-two years ago, when he was in the flower of his youth. He was a strong young man, robust and beautiful. He had a happy and pleasant disposition, and he could always be found in the company of friends, when his activities and business allowed for this. Nature gifted him with a magnificent contralto voice. He was always ready to sing for the delight and solace of every social gathering and to add his voice to inspiring religious devotions when he joined the church choir. He was a gentle and ardent husband and a loving parent. He dedicated all his energy to the well-being and comfort of the very large family Divine Providence had entrusted to his care and guardianship. And being that he was a poor man, he rarely ever permitted himself to enjoy even the simplest of pleasures, out of duty to his loved ones who depended on him.

He was always loyal and faithful to his friends, of which there were many, as so many of you attending this funeral have had the opportunity to see. His balanced, clear mind and judgment made him a trusted confidant to many who looked to him for counsel and guidance in personal matters and in public dealings. He was a descendent of an old and distinguished lineage. He had enough pride to keep his family crest clean and without stain. His word was his bond, and any promise he willingly made, if it was in his power to keep it, could be redeemed and guaranteed. His sense of duty in public as in private life knew no point of compromise or middle ground; rather for him it meant that he must keep all his commitments and nothing less. Any move to induce him to pull away from his promise out of convenience went nowhere. To sum up, when Governor Baca found the right path of duty, and once he had resolved this in any matter, he was able to say, as the knights of old had done, "First will this rock fly away from where it now sits before I move."

At no time, quite likely, over the course of his life did he show the solidity of his character more visibly and energetically than in his last political campaign. When he was called by his political friends to head up the Democratic ballot. He already knew this endeavor would cost him his life, but he also was aware that his party needed him and had sought him out as a leader. He believed it was his duty to answer the call of his party, and true to himself and to the traditions of his family, like Caesar standing on the banks of the Rubicon,[93] he said, "The die has been cast," and he prepared himself for battle.

While, dear friends, at a first reception last October, at the request of the central committee of the Republican Party, I needed to go to Española[94] to give a speech before the Republican County Convention set to meet there that day. It was raining, and it was cold and not at all pleasant. Around noon, Governor Baca and his entourage came by automobile to the hotel where I was staying. The governor was bundled up in a heavy coat. He took careful, slow steps. His face was flushed, and he plainly showed signs of fatigue. It was painful to see him. I took his hand and said, "Dear friend, I think you are very imprudent." He answered, "This is likely so, but it must be done." These words fully explain what kind of man he was.

Ladies and gentlemen, such was the man that a free people elevated to the high post of chief executive of our state. He had within him the elements of greatness, and he was not exempt from the tests and tribulations that sometimes sour the lives of great men. He had many enemies, but they could be seen alongside his friends tossing flowers on his grave, a gesture meant to clear away the many thorns that they had managed to cast across his via dolorosa as he journeyed on earth. As is the case with many great men, he was a poor man. And like the great lawmaker of Israel, he guided his people to the edge of the promised land, but also like the great patriarch, he was not able to enjoy the great jubilee. Sick and near death, he took the oath of office in the chamber for those with debilitating health in this city. He was never to leave that room and there undertook a valiant struggle against death, the destroyer of life, disputing every inch of ground, until at last, the angel of death sounded the trumpet call and he, like a pristine flower that lowers its beautiful corolla, draped in the covers of his bed, reclined back as if into a pleasant dream and left behind forever the site of his efforts and of his brilliant victories. He was a martyr for his people in carrying out his public charge. The final step in this drama intensified, when, as if determined by Divine Providence, the silent and respectful procession accompanying the body of the deceased governor came into view and with it his daughter, Adelina. Her insistent questioning about where her father had gone had been answered by telling her that he had left on a long journey. When she saw the procession nearing, she clapped her small hands and in sweet and prodigious simplicity said, "Good, oh very good, there comes my father." May God bless this innocent child!

With the death of Governor Baca, his family and the state have incurred a great loss, a loss that is doubly painful given the circumstances in which it occurred. Yet Divine Providence, ever merciful, ever watchful over the fate of men, orders all things for the good and provided a successor to the deceased governor. Given his knowledge and patriotism, he is a man in whom we can all be entirely confident. While Divine Providence does not, even for an instant, lose sight of the defenseless children who are left to lament the loss of a generous and loving father, it is comforting to know that the honorable representatives of the state in session here in this city have taken necessary measures to protect the interests of the family and guard it against need. This is a good and well-executed action.

The state of New Mexico is large, and it is quite correct to see that the widow and children of any of its governors are not subject to privations and destitution.

In conclusion, my friends, as the state of New Mexico is as grand as any other state, let its great people be an equally grateful community. Spartacus built a monument at Thermopylae dedicated to Leonidas[95] and to the handful of warriors that turned back the Xerxes with their legions. On that monument a grateful people inscribed these words: "Go forth, traveler, and tell Spartacus that all have willingly died in obedience to his sacred laws." Likewise, on the gravestone marking the final resting place of the departed Governor Baca, let us be an equally grateful people and inscribe on that epitaph, "Go forth, traveler, and tell the world that I have died here on the altar of my duty to the homeland."

Notes to the Translation

1. The original text was transcribed from the facsimile reproduced in Twitchell 75–76.

2. Throughout the text, Vigil y Alarid strives to maintain his composure, opting to be evenhanded and levelheaded even as he faces a most deleterious circumstance. Here, however, he employs the Spanish word *tropel* to refer to Kearny's army. The Spanish term is the word for "throng," literally a crowd that moves in an unorganized, strepitous, boisterous way. By so doing, Vigil y Alarid takes back what the translation renders as "the strict discipline of your troops." The dig, no doubt, was obvious to his fellow Nuevomexicanos.

3. Vigil y Alarid alludes to the situation in Poland after dispositions made at the Congress of Vienna of 1815 reorganized the map of Europe at the end of the Napoleonic Wars and permitted Russia to take over large portions of Poland, with devastating results for the Polish people.

4. Over a hundred species of nopal, or prickly pear cactus, are known in Mexico. Nopales are commonly used in Mexican cuisine. Because of their ubiquitous presence in homes and markets, they are regarded as an emblematic symbol of Mexicanness, in the way Chacón references the plant here.

5. La Malinche is also known as Malintzín in Nahuatl and by her Christian name, Marina. She was one of several women tributed to Spaniards in 1519 and is known for her role as an interpreter, intermediary, and advisor to the Spanish conquistador Hernán Cortez. As a consort to Cortez, she birthed children who came to be regarded as the first mestizos, or mixed-raced peoples, of New Spain, or present-day Mexico. Here Chacón evokes La Malinche and Cortez as the central figures in one of the most dramatic episodes in the history of Mexico.

6. Chacón's reference is to the Battle of Puebla, fought at Puebla, Mexico, on 5 May 1862, where Mexican forces defeated an interventionary force of French troops sent by Napoleon III to establish a French government in Mexico. This victory became a symbol of resistance to foreign domination and gave rise to the annual Cinco de Mayo celebrations that commemorate the victory.

7. In the Spanish original, Chacón uses the Portuguese "Mavorte" instead of the Spanish "Marte" to allude to the god of war in Roman mythology, an interesting example of the author's penchant for lexical complexity.

8. A reference to the Treaty of Miramar, signed on 10 April 1864 between France and Mexico, which stipulated a gradual reduction of French troops and called for their eventual withdrawal from Mexico. It would be another three years before Napoleon Bonaparte would give up on his quest to establish an empire in Mexico.

9. As the wife of the Austrian archduke Maximilian, Carlota accompanied her husband when he accepted the crown as emperor of Mexico that was offered to him in 1864 by Napoleon III. Carlota is viewed as a sympathetic figure in Mexican history for her effort to learn Spanish and for her genuine interest in Mexican history, art, and culture.

10. The Roman goddess of agriculture, green crops, fertility, and motherhood.

11. A name derived from Latin and introduced to Mexico by the Spanish. It refers to the genus of monocots indigenous to the Americas. The plant holds a central place in Mexican culture. *Agave azul*, or blue agave, is used in the production of mezcal, from which derives a distilled form of drink best known as tequila. In Aztec mythology the plant is associated with the story of the goddess Mayahuel, who was transformed into the maguey plant. The spires of the maguey dot the landscape of Mexico. The ubiquitous presence of the plant has come to symbolize passion and transformation ("Legend"; "Agave").

12. In 2023 the University of New Mexico's Center for Southwest Research and Special Collections borrowed the original cassette tapes from the Las Vegas Carnegie Public Library and digitized them. The interviews are now available for listening as a result of a collaboration between the Center for Southwest Research and Special Collections, the University of New Mexico's Digital Initiatives and Scholarly Communication program, and the Las Vegas Carnegie Public Library.

13. Espinosa was born in 1880 in Carnero, Colorado, into a family of Nuevomexicano farmers and ranchers descended from the early Spanish-Mexican settlers of New Mexico. After completing his bachelor's degree, he took a teaching position at the University of New Mexico for a short time until enrolling at the University of Chicago in 1907. In 1909 he completed his doctorate in Romance languages. In the same year he joined the faculty of the Department of Romance Languages at Stanford University, where he remained a professor until 1958 (Nieto-Phillips 179).

14. Pulling together the recollections of his informants, Espinosa was only able to deduce that Vilmas was held up to be the Nuevomexicano maestro of the *trova* and that Gracia and the Black Poet

were junior rivals who continually challenged Vilmas, hoping to dethrone him. Espinosa could not determine when these two troubadours lived or even if they were real persons. Considerably more is known about the Black Poet. Often referred to as the *negro poeta mexicano* (the black Mexican poet), researchers have concluded that he was born in the area of Puebla, Mexico, to a Congolese family. His fame as a troubadour spread in colonial New Spain, where he became known for the biting sarcasm of his improvised verses, many of which dealt with his position in society as an Afro-mestizo.

15. The opening verse of this *trova* places the encounter of the two maestros of legend in the township of Oposura. This detail is remarkable since it refers to a real location, San Miguel Arcángel de Oposura, in the present Mexican state of Sonora. San Miguel Arcángel de Oposura began as a mission church founded by the Jesuit Marcos del Río in 1644. Throughout the colonial period, the mission was known simply as Oposura. After Mexican independence the town was renamed Moctezuma in honor of the Mexican soldier and politician Francisco Moctezuma.

16. A person from Zihuatanejo, a town in the Mexican state of Guerrero.

17. Refers to the thirty pieces of silver mentioned in the Gospel of Matthew that Judas Iscariot received for his betrayal of Christ.

18. A double entendre results from the homophone *ave*, which in Spanish can mean "bird" or the salutation "hail," as in "hail Mary."

19. Espinosa only references this individual as Gracia and not as Gracia Istavera or Tavera, as happens in Francisco Sena's *trova* (entry 3), where Gracia is uniformly presented as another one of Old Man Vilmas's rivals. Additionally, his appearance not only alludes to the idea of grace in theological or religious terms but also can refer to wit *(tener gracia)*, hilarity *(hacer gracia)*, or elegance *(demostrar gracia)*.

20. Refers to the three Graces of Greek mythology, which represent three forms of ideal female beauty.

21. A major figure in the Old Testament. He is credited with building the first Temple of Jerusalem and was revered for his wisdom and just decision-making.

22. Jacob and Rachel are two figures in the Old Testament. As the story goes, Jacob was forced by his father-in-law to marry Leah, although he was secretly in love with her sister Rachel. Fourteen years passed before he could be with Rachel.

23. There are several figures in Greek and Roman mythology by this name. In many accounts, this female goddess is associated with wisdom, courage, beauty, and inspiration.

24. Helen of Troy in Greek mythology. She was known for her beauty and said to have been the cause of the Trojan War.

25. Known as the penitent thief mentioned in the New Testament and one of two men who were crucified alongside Christ.

26. The mother of Solomon and David, heirs to Judean kingship. Bathsheba was adept at maneuvering her way through the intricacies and intrigues of the court. She eventually managed to have Solomon ascend to the throne of Israel despite his being younger than David.

27. Said to have been the son of King David and Abigail, although some held that Chileab was not fathered by David but that God had arranged for Chileab to bear a resemblance to David.

28. Pharez, also written as *Perez*, appears in the Book of Genesis. He is the son of Judah and Tamar and the twin brother of Zerah. The biblical account has it that Tamar seduced her father-in-law by disguising herself as a prostitute.

29. A reference from the Book of Esther in the Old Testament. Ahasuerus, Esther's husband, is said to have ruled over many regions from India to Nubia.

30. One of the three wise men depicted in the New Testament. Known as the King of Arabia, he is said to have brought the gift of myrrh to Jesus. The allusion to the pharaoh in the prior verse appears to conflate the despotic rule of the ancient rulers of Egypt with Herod, the king of Judea at the time of the birth of Jesus.

31. Appears in Greek mythology as a figure in the Trojan War and other legends. At the time of the Trojan War, he takes up with Helena. Their elopement brought about the conflict.

32. Roman emperor from 284 until his abdication in 307. He was separated from his wife, Prisca, when he retired.

33. Ushered in the age of Charlemagne when he became emperor of the Holy Roman Empire in 800 CE. His reputation as a model king who ruled by virtue and principle is belied by his complicated relationships with women. He had eighteen children with seven of ten known wives or concubines. He famously forbade his daughters from marrying during his lifetime.

34. *Freire* is a word in Portuguese and Galician referring to the vocation of friar and applied to an outwardly pious person or, by extension, to someone employed in a monastery. There is the extremely

complicated history of the Freire family and a number of intermarriages in the border region of Galicia and Portugal. These unions led in equally complex ways to the central role played by Freires in the creation of a twelfth-century military order organized to battle the Muslims on the Iberian Peninsula.

35. Nuevomexicanos referred to the tributary known today as the Canadian River as the *río Colorado*, or "Colorado River." They adopted this name since the river began in Colorado, traversed northeastern New Mexico, and continued on into the Texas and Oklahoma panhandle.

36. The troubadour was apt to insert the name of the town where the ballad was being performed as a way to make the story more relevant to those in the audience.

37. The name of this lesser-known bard is associated with the chicory plant and its woody, rough stem and bitter taste. More often seen as a wild-growing weed, it was primarily used as forage for animals. Espinosa does not mention Chicoria in his 1914 article, but we can assume that like other bards he had acquired a certain amount of fame in the region.

38. For more on the Black Poet, see note 14.

39. A second lieutenant at the outset of the Mexican-American War, Logan was stationed in Santa Fe but saw no action. He subsequently served as a general during the American Civil War and later played a key role in the establishment of Memorial Day as a national holiday. He died in 1886, four years before the publication of "Poor Emilio." Presumably, Padilla is recounting Logan's appearance at the Lamy station on a return visit to New Mexico while he was serving as a US senator from Illinois and had his eye on the presidency. Unfortunately, he succumbed to an unexpected illness in middle age, a circumstance that may explain Padilla's description of him as a "gallant but unfortunate patriot."

40. In the Spanish text, Padilla employs the expression "no había pagado atención," a direct borrowing of the English verb "to pay." The standard Spanish expression makes use of the verb "prestar" and would render the phrase as "no había prestado atención." Earlier, Padilla uses a direct borrowing of the English word "depot" and renders it as "dipo" in the Spanish, as was common in this period.

41. Padilla uses the term "yanqui," or "Yankee," as it was employed at the end of the nineteenth century to refer to a northerner or someone native to New England.

42. Heinrich Heine (1797–1856), a German Romantic poet who came to international fame for his 1827 *The Book of Songs*, which con-

tained poems that were often set to music. In seeking a civil service job closed to Jews, Heine opted to convert to Protestantism but did so with little enthusiasm and some resentment.

43. The most famous of the one-eyed giants described in Greek mythology. The son of Poseidon, the god of the sea, and the nymph Thoösa.

44. A reference to the global flood described in Genesis, the first book of the Bible. Also known as Noah's flood.

45. The organizations named reflect the Great Captain's admiration for groups and programs of action that agitated against order and social convention through revolutionary activism. Russian nihilism considered all morality, religion, and established social institutions meaningless and irrelevant; the Italian Mafia operated in American cities, ostensibly as a mutual aid association, but often devolved into criminal activity; the Indiana White Caps engaged in vigilante activities in southern Indiana following the American Civil War; the Chicago anarchists rejected the concept of private property and organized government; the Knights of Labor, an early labor federation, worked to organize railroad workers, miners, and others to improve working conditions.

46. Nuevomexicanos ascribed the term *nativo* ("native") to themselves soon after the arrival of Anglo-Americans in the region. In taking up the term, they were not defining themselves against the Native Americans as First Peoples; rather, they began to define themselves against Anglo-American waves of immigrants arriving in the second half of the nineteenth century. In addition to referring to themselves as Mexican, they made use of the fuller terms *colono nativo* or *paisano native* ("native settler" or "countryman") as a shield against the external, extraneous, foreign settler—the *extranjero* or *inmigrante* (Otero et al. xvi).

47. In his definitive study on captivity and exchange between Spanish New Mexicans and indigenous tribes, the historian James F. Brooks points out how "borderland cultural and political economies bound indigenous and colonial peoples in long-term relations of violence, exchange, interdependence, and inter-development" (31). Brooks concludes that the intercultural violence between the Nuevomexicanos and native groups is best described as "a chaotic and unceasing predatory war" (35).

48. Salazar refers to Zebulon Pike and John C. Frémont. Pike is best known for leading an exploration party for the US government from St. Louis, Missouri, to explore the headwaters of the Mississippi River in 1805. At the start of the Mexican-American War,

Frémont, a military officer and mapmaker, operated along the Pacific coast. He and his followers defied Mexican authorities prior to the start of the war in northern California, and he eventually supported an uprising against Mexican rule known as the Bear Flag Revolt in 1846.

49. The tendency in certain writers and historians to demonize the Spanish Empire and minimize Spanish achievements by fostering a distorted view of the history of Spain, particularly of its colonization of Latin America and other regions, with the intent of undercutting its standing in world affairs.

50. The literal translation of the Spanish title would be "The Truth without a Shawl about New Mexico." I have chosen to offer this more idiomatic translation of the title.

51. See note 46 for a discussion of the term *nativo* ("native") as it was used by Nuevomexicanos.

52. The principal actors in the cause for Mexican independence from Spanish rule beginning in 1810.

53. Although generally undervalued when compared to other American Civil War battles, New Mexico was the scene of two important conflicts: the Battle of Valverde, which took place in southern New Mexico in February 1862, and a second engagement that took place at Glorieta Pass, twenty miles southeast of Santa Fe, in March 1862.

54. Movements advocating statehood rose and waned at various points in the six decades after the US takeover of New Mexico. The election of 1890 is one of several attempts to promote statehood through popular referendum. In this instance, Nuevomexicanos like Sena joined with local business associations and entrepreneurs to support moves to enable the drafting of a constitution in support of New Mexico's bid for statehood (Holtby 7).

55. Prior to large-scale, mechanized agricultural farming, made possible by reclamation projects in southern New Mexico and other parts of the West, Mora County was touted as the "bread basket of New Mexico." The county produced large harvests of corn, wheat, barley, oats, and potatoes that supplied Fort Union and other military posts. At one time there were seven active water-powered mills on a seventy-mile stretch of the Mora River ("Mora County"). The village of Mora had also been bombed by a contingent of US forces sent from Santa Fe to put down the Taos Revolt in January 1847 (McNierney 35–46). By the time New Mexico became a state, and as Lucero's report demonstrates, later generations of Nuevomexicanos were in full sympathy with the notion of joining in the defense of the nation.

56. Washington Ellsworth Lindsey was born in Ohio in 1862. He attended the University of Michigan, where he earned his law degree. He moved to New Mexico around 1900, where he continued his law practice and engaged in New Mexico politics. He was a member of the state constitutional convention and assumed the duties of governor of the state upon the death of Ezequiel Cabeza de Baca (entry 31) in February 1917.

57. Judge David Leahy presided over the Fourth Judicial District of New Mexico, which encompassed Mora County, San Miguel County, and Guadalupe County, areas with large Hispanic populations.

58. Octaviano A. Larrazolo (entry 31).

59. C. W. G. Ward was at the time the district attorney of neighboring San Miguel County.

60. A. C. Voorhees was a progressive active in Republican politics. He would later run for the US Senate in 1924.

61. A moniker for New Mexico that was popular at the time but that would later lose out to the more common referent "the Land of Enchantment."

62. A reference to the sinking of the British-owned ocean liner the *Lusitania* by a German submarine off the coast of Ireland on 7 May 1915. Some 1,195 passengers died as a result. The sinking of the *Lusitania* came to be seen as a blatant transgression of the conventions of war and was the act that led to the entrance of the United States into World War I.

63. Chacón refers to Brno, a city within the Austro-Hungarian Empire at the outset of World War I. Brno had a sizeable Jewish population with a history that reached back to the thirteenth century. The Jewish community of Brno was highly integrated into local society and sided with the Austro-Hungarian Empire during World War I.

64. Chacón footnotes his poem at this point, indicating that *Usona* is "[v]oz compuesta de las letras iniciales de United States of North America, con las misma significación" ("a word comprised of the initial letters of the United States of North America, and bearing the same meaning").

65. Mount Belleau, also known as Belleau Wood, is some fifty miles from Paris. In 1918 it became the site of a protracted battle between the US Marines and German forces. While small in comparison to other actions at the time, the battle occupies an important place in the annals of US military history, signaling an early display of capabilities by the American Expeditionary Forces on the battlefield. German officers began to refer to the marines as "devil dogs," a name that has come to be a celebrated symbol.

66. A reference to Kaiser William II, who is charged with turning conflicts between Germany and France into the world conflict that World War I would become. By failing to challenge the grandiose war plans of his generals, the German army proceeded to attack cities and towns in Belgium and France at the outset of World War I.

67. Nero Claudius Caesar Augustus Germanicus was a Roman emperor and the final emperor of the Julio-Claudian dynasty, reigning from 54 BCE until his death in 68 BCE.

68. For more on Diocletian, see note 32.

69. Roman goddess of war.

70. A heartfelt cry of lament expressing deep sorrow and anguish. The expression is from the Latin for "from the depths."

71. Here the student-poet offers a playful take on her name, which traditionally derives from an advocation to the Virgin Mary in the guise of La Virgen de los Remedios (Our Lady of Remedies). The play on words results from the additional meaning of her name as "remedy" or "cure."

72. A designation at the time for colleges that specialized in preparing students for the teaching profession.

73. Gonzales is acknowledging the work of the Jesuits who over a period of several decades had managed to recruit a number of young Nuevomexicanos through a feeder network of schools to study at St. Louis University.

74. "Vervoritis" is a made-up word, a combination of *verbo*, meaning "word"—which the author of this piece, perhaps purposefully, misspells as "vervo"—and the Latin suffix *-itis*. The combination suggests the condition of a widespread, common infirmity, an affliction, in this case, of drivel.

75. Throughout the translation, italics indicate the use of English expressions in the original Spanish text.

76. These lyrics are from a popular song titled "I Want Yer, Ma Honey." While the lyrics mimic black vernacular speech, they were composed by Fay Templeton, a white composer, and were likely performed in minstrel fashion. That the lyrics appear in this dialogue is another sign that the speakers are aware of and influenced by current popular trends in American life.

77. Throughout the translation, italics indicate the use of English expressions in the original Spanish text. Where necessary, clarifications are provided in brackets.

78. A reference to William Howard Taft, the twenty-seventh president of the United States, who served in office from 1909 to 1913.

79. This expression is a deliberate ethnic slur reflecting anti-Asian sentiments in both the United States and Mexico. The diffusion of it can be attributed to the staging of the play *Chin Chun Chan: Conflicto chino en un acto y tres cuadras (Chin Chun Chan: A Chinese Conflict in One Act and Three Blocks)* in Mexico City in 1904. Chinese migration to northern Mexico at the time fueled virulent anti-Chinese campaigns in the press (Buffington).

80. A local mercantile store, known for its fashionable merchandise.

81. A reference to the destructive power of the German war machine. Germany was the first country to employ submarines in war, and its decision to use them against merchant ships on the open sea caused fear in the general public.

82. The foremost and most highly acclaimed writers and dramatists of Spanish Golden Age literature.

83. The word *comfortable* appears in quotation marks in the original Spanish text, drawing attention to the fact that Ortiz means to voice the cognate in English as a subtle dig meant to parody the insistent use of the word in the speech of newcomers to Santa Fe who go about displaying their high status and concerns.

84. This piece first appeared in *La Revista de Taos (The Taos Review)* on 31 October 1913 and was reprinted the following month in *El Nuevo Mexicano*.

85. "Pero Grullo" is a combination of "Pero" (an archaic form of "Peter") and "grullo," a long-winded talker, or someone with the gift of gab. The name is most often associated with oral literature and the popular classes and is referenced in Spain as early as the fifteenth century.

86. George Curry served as governor of the New Mexico territory between 1907 and 1910.

87. A direct genealogical tie between Ezequiel Cabeza de Baca and Álvar Núñez Cabeza de Vaca, the explorer-trekker, is improbable, given that Cabeza de Vaca left Mexico City for Spain in 1537. In time, he was awarded a governorship for an area that overlapped present-day borders of Paraguay, Uruguay, and Argentina. There his leadership was characterized by his benign treatment of several Indian communities. Reséndez notes that he was a "curious leader, who behaved more like a missionary than a conquistador" (230). It is reasonable to assume that the Cabeza de Baca family name made its way to New Mexico sometime after the explorer's death in 1559.

88. A reference to a legend that circulated in sixteenth-century New Spain that spoke of the existence of seven golden cities reputed to be in the area of present-day New Mexico and Arizona.

89. An eleventh-century French monk and ascetic, Peter the Hermit founded monasteries before setting off to Jerusalem with the First Crusade. Known as an electrifying preacher, he preached a sermon on the Mount of Olives prior to the storming of Jerusalem by Christian forces in 1099.

90. Larrazolo's enumeration of Spanish-led expeditions into New Mexico between 1539 and 1598 is historically accurate. Speculation about the lands lying to the north of Mexico City were fueled by Álvar Núñez Cabeza de Vaca's initial reports, and in time legends were grafted onto his accounts by later explorers. For example, when the friar and expedition leader Marcos de Niza edged up to Zuni Pueblo in southwestern New Mexico in 1539, members of his party caught sight of the sun reflecting on the mud- and mica-filled walls of the Indian villages and imagined walls glittering with gold leaf. Upon their return to Mexico City, their tale gave rise to the myth of the Seven Cities of Cíbola and to the idea that towns made of gold could be found in the region. The Juan de Oñate expedition of 1598 established the first permanent European settlement in North America.

91. Refers to political alliances headed by the three most powerful public figures in ancient Roman society. At any given time and across generations, several such groupings in ancient Rome emerged and held power over the state.

92. See note 78.

93. Refers to a shallow river in northeastern Italy that was famously crossed by Julius Caesar in 49 BCE. The expression "crossing the Rubicon" has come to mean crossing a point of no return.

94. A town in Rio Arriba County in central New Mexico, a midpoint between Santa Fe and Taos, New Mexico.

95. A reference to ancient Greece and to a battle at a mountain pass in central Greece called Thermopylae. There, in 480 BCE, Spartan forces led by Leonidas were outflanked by the Persian army commanded by Xerxes. The battle came to symbolize heroic resistance in the face of overwhelming odds.

Works Cited in the Notes to the Translation

"Agave." *Wikipedia*, 15 Aug. 2024, en.wikipedia.org/wiki/Agave.

Brooks, James F. *Captives and Cousins: Slavery, Kinship and Community in the Southwest Borderlands.* U of North Carolina P, 2002.

Buffington, Robert M. "Chin, Chun, Chan: Popular Sinophobia in Early Twentieth Century Mexico City." *The Americas*, vol. 78, no. 2, Apr. 2021. pp. 279–318.

Espinosa, Aurelio M. "New Mexico Spanish Folklore." *The Journal of American Folklore*, vol. 27, no. 104, April-June 1914, pp. 105–47.

Holtby, David V. *Forty-Seventh Star: New Mexico's Struggle for Statehood.* U of Oklahoma P, 2012.

"The Legend of the Goddess Mayahuel in Aztec Mythology." *Experience Mayahuel*, experiencemayahuel.com/legend-goddess -mayahuel-aztec-mythology/. Accessed 15 Aug. 2024.

McNierney, Michael, editor. *Taos 1847: The Revolt in Contemporary Accounts.* Johnson Publishing, 1980.

"Mora County—Her Reputation as 'the Granary of New Mexico' Makes Her a Most Desirable County in Which to Locate." *El Mosquito*, vol. 1, no. 2, 3 Dec. 1891, p. 4.

Nieto-Phillips, John. *The Language of Blood: The Making of Spanish American Identity in the Southwest.* U of New Mexico P, 2004.

Otero, Rosalie C., et al., editors. *Santa Fe Nativa: A Collection of Nuevomexicano Writing.* U of New Mexico P, 2009.

Reséndez, Andrés. *A Land So Strange: The Epic Journey of Cabeza de Vaca.* Basic Books, 2007.

Twitchell, Ralph Emerson. *The History of the Military Occupation of the Territory of New Mexico from 1846 to 1851 by the Government of the United States.* Smith-Brooks, 1909.

About the Translator

A. Gabriel Meléndez is distinguished professor of American studies (retired) at the University of New Mexico and a specialist in the recovery of the literature and thought of early Mexican Americans in the US-Mexico borderlands. He has written and edited a number of books, including *So All Is Not Lost: The Poetics of Print in Nuevomexicano Communities, 1834–1958* (1997), *The Multicultural Southwest: A Reader* (2001), *Santa Fe Nativa: A Collection of Nuevomexicano Writing* (2010), *Hidden Chicano Cinema: Film Dramas in the Borderlands* (2013), and, with Anna Nogar, *El feliz ingenio neomexicano: Felipe M. Chacón and* Poesía y prosa (2021).